C000149372

Motivated

The Reluctant Leader's Guide to building a business that sets you free

Mark Terrell

Dear Amal

Wishing you a

Motivated 2022

Mark

Published by The Book Chief Publishing House 2021
(a trademark under Lydian Group Ltd)
Suite 2A, Blackthorn House, St Paul's Square, Birmingham, B3
1RL
www.thebookchief.com

The moral right of the author has been asserted.

Text Copyright 2021 by **Mark Terrell**

All rights reserved. No part of this book may be reproduced, stored
in a retrieval system, or transmitted in any form or by any means,
electronic, mechanical, photocopying, recording, public
performances or otherwise, without written permission of Mark
Terrell, except for brief quotations embodied in critical articles or
reviews. The book is for personal use only; commercial use is
prohibited unless written permission and a license is obtained from
the author **Mark Terrell.**

The right of Mark Terrell to be identified as the author of this work
has been asserted in accordance with sections 77 and 78 of the
copyright Designs and Patents Act 1988.

Book Cover Design / Illustrations: Deearo Marketing
Editor: Laura Billingham
Typesetting / Publishing: Sharon Brown
Proofreaders: Sharon Brown / Laura Billingham

THE BOOK CHIEF

IGNITE YOUR WRITING

Table of Contents

Dedication

To Hayley and Emily, there are many paths you can take, whichever you choose, make sure it's your path and follow your heart.

Foreword

By James Sale

I have known Mark Terrell now for over 20 years. When we first met, he was my Investors in People client for his successful retail business in Chippenham. Right from the start I realised that Mark was a learning sponge, that he loved everything to do with people, people development, and included in that was his own development. In the time I have known him, he has made incredible strides in this area, and alongside that, of course, he has acquired massive knowledge, advanced skills, and huge experience to draw on in order to write this book.

And, unsurprisingly, the book is a wonderful compendium: it advocates developing energy (aka motivation) at all costs, it provides fabulous and relevant stories drawn from his vast experience and success, it highlights the tools you need to become effective, it draws on a wide range of reading and literature without at any point becoming 'academic' and tedious, it is ideas-rich; and in short if you just implemented three ideas from the dozens available on these pages, you would still get a 100x return from your investment in buying it!

The book is also deeply personal. One notes with interest the 'ghost' of his father - his original mentor and role model - as he pops up in one confidential anecdote after another. But it is clear to me, even if Mark doesn't say it, he has gone further than his father ever could - and if his father were alive today, he would be mightily proud of his son. This is an example to us all: whoever our role model is, to go beyond what they achieved and to create new successes in areas where they never even dreamed to go.

Mark has become his own man, and this book is so powerful precisely because it is so personal. Yet ... his ideas and advice are there for all to use.

So, I heartily recommend this book to you. It is hard won - from the fiery furnace of experience and the long labours of study. It is perhaps one of the best books I have come across that succinctly enables a business owner to get on top of their business and to enable it to thrive. I sincerely hope this book sells thousands of copies - it deserves to. If you read it, make sure you recommend it to a friend or colleague!

Acknowledgements

Thank you to all those who helped to bring this book to life, Joe Gregory and Lucy McCarraher at Book Builder, James and Linda Sale at Motivational Maps, my Beta Readers Ali Stewart, Bevis Moynan, Adrian Chase and Miles Kitching.

Introduction

This book is all about energy, to manage our energy levels we need to know what gives us energy and what saps our energy. Like fuel in the car, motivation is the energy we need to keep going, which needs to be topped up with the right type that's not going to evaporate overnight.

When you started out you were full of energy to create a business that could give you the life you always dreamt of. You had some technical knowledge, were good at what you did and working for someone else just wasn't cutting it anymore.

Initially, things go well, your turnover is growing and everything feels like it's going in the right direction. It's hard work but doesn't feel like it as you are now calling the shots and doing things your way.

You have employed people to expand your capacity and to free up your time, but that's not really worked out, you're working harder than ever. Then there's the added responsibility that comes with having a team to think about and how to get the best from each of them.

After 30 years of working in my family's retail business and then selling to a national retailer, I was able to spend time reflecting on what went well and what didn't. I reached the position of leading the business, not from a desire to be in charge, but from being someone who could see opportunities to improve the business by innovating and introducing new ideas.

I had never had any formal leadership training, so I led using my own intuition and was successful in that we had low staff turnover and the business continued to grow in a very competitive market. We won a number of industry awards and also gained Investors in People recognition which was a particularly proud moment.

I mentioned our focus on innovation which involved being at the forefront of convenience store development in the UK when we began to trade seven days per week. We were also one of the early adopters of electronic point of sale in the independent sector and fully computerised our back office systems.

Retail is a great way to learn about business and how important it is to keep one step ahead of the competition. I learnt how to keep the customer as the key focus and also how important a great team is to business success.

Having been there and knowing how it feels to be in charge and the responsibility that it brings, I can empathise with the financial and emotional challenges. It's so easy to fall into the trap of getting ground down by people issues and lose sight of the goals of the business.

What I've noticed when working with my clients is that their troubles stem from either not wanting to be in charge, or not having the know-how to lead a team or a combination of both. There is an adage that says leaders are born, not made, which is nonsense. Anyone can learn to lead a team, they just need to decide they want to.

Not wanting to be in charge is often linked to a focus on other things, or in other words, it is way down the list of priorities, and subsequently, it is done badly or not at all. We tend to focus our time on what motivates us, so if managing people doesn't motivate you and something else does, then that's where your focus will be.

If not addressed, a lack of focus on leading, managing and developing your team will lead to the problems of having an unhappy, disengaged, and unproductive team. Your time will then be taken up dealing with low morale, and you'll wonder why you bothered employing people at all.

I've combined my own experience of these problems and some tools and techniques I learnt since selling my business to create a solution that will give you what you need to get the M.E.A.S.U.R.E of your business. The starting point is establishing what you want from your business so you can create the role that suits you and then build everything from there.

What I will take you through in this book is a step by step approach to creating the business you always wanted, one that motivates and works for you and not the other way around. The essential element is you, keeping you highly motivated and knowing how to focus on the key skills to develop a team to run the business day to day.

Not only will you create a business that's enjoyable to run, it will also be more attractive to potential buyers if you ever want to sell. You may think you need to be the biggest cog in the machine when in actual fact you need to be the oil that keeps it running smoothly.

Performance is a buzzword in self-development which grates on me a little, I prefer to focus on motivation which is one of three components of performance that often gets overlooked. Motivation is essentially why we do things, our motive to take action, so it's important to understand what is really motivating us so we can make aligned decisions.

If you find leadership theory confusing and sometimes irrelevant to you, I know how you feel. My intention with this book is to clarify all the steps you need to take so you know why they are important and also how they are dependent on each other.

I wanted to write this book because the majority of the leadership books I come across are focused on the corporate arena rather than the small to medium-sized businesses that really need it. Most businesses are started by someone who wanted to have more control over their time and use their specialist knowledge to make a bigger difference in the world.

The reality is that most business owners end up working more hours for less income and running a business that takes over their lives. I don't want that to happen to you, I want you to create a business that works for you by showing you the steps to take and the pitfalls to avoid.

By recognising the three elements that need to work together, you, the business and your team, you can then have a strategy that fits each element and also serves the overall vision. My intention is to inspire you to embrace your role in leading your business and your team, enjoy the journey and, most importantly, stay motivated!

PART ONE: MOTIVATED YOU

Let's start with the most important element. You!

Your focus should be to be the most motivated person in the business so you are in the best position to lead. In Part One of the book, we will look at the factors that affect your energy, motivation being one of them, how to identify what's really driving you and then making sure you have a plan in place that will keep you at your most productive.

CHAPTER 1:

Business Should Be a Lifestyle Not Your Life

Introduction

So, what made you think starting a business was a good idea? Oh yeah, you thought it couldn't be that difficult judging by all those idiots you've been working for, and if they can do it, why can't you. The chances are it wasn't all down to logic, a majority was down to a motive, a motive to take action, motivation.

What was your motive? Was it to make more money, have more freedom, more security or make a difference in the world? As time goes by and as our commitment to the business increases, it's easy to forget what it was because we now relate more to our current circumstances.

Take a moment to reconnect with that decision and what you might be doing if you hadn't made it, hopefully this has confirmed it was the right decision. The business owner or entrepreneur's lifestyle is not for everyone, but once made, it's all about embracing the opportunities that it brings.

This chapter is about creating the right environment that will give you the best possible chance of success.

Enjoy the journey – don't become a work victim

Setting goals is important, and I'm going to show you how you can set the right ones for you and your business later on in the book. Goals are a way to check in with your progress and allow you to celebrate once you have achieved them, but they are not the be all and end all.

It's just as important to appreciate the road to achieving those goals how we react and learn from the twists and turns will be just as valuable as the eventual outcome. Our attitude plays a big part in how we react to our circumstances, and sometimes we just need to stop and give ourselves time to think and breathe.

If we get too transfixed on future goals, we can easily lose touch with what's going on around us and start to live in our own world based on achievement only. It's often said that we can be overly optimistic when it comes to what we can achieve short term, but the opposite is true in the long term.

Simon Tyler wrote 'The Attitude Book', and in it, he defines attitude as "*The choice, conscious or unconscious, to hold yourself in thought, mind and body in relation to anything that shows up*". He goes on to say, "*for most people, it is about letting circumstances influence and set their attitude – in which case we get hurled around by the winds of our life and imminent impact with the ground of reality*".

We can choose the attitude we take to the circumstances that are thrown at us. There's no more sobering moment than when we feel that everything is against us, and then a hearse drives by. Finding ways to put things into perspective can keep us focused on what's important. One way I've found is following those who document their fight against cancer on social media, not knowing if there is a future will keep you focused on the present

One way to stay present and make sure you are noticing each step you are making is to use a journal. Journaling is a great way of getting what's bouncing around in your head down on paper so you can return to it later. It will give you a point of reference when you look back at particularly challenging times and may even become the basis to write a book.

There will inevitably be times when you need to have strategies to keep yourself in a good place to make important decisions. When things get a bit stressful, I notice my breathing gets a bit short and shallow, when I notice this happening, I take a moment to focus on my breathing.

A simple technique I was taught is the 4:4:4 system which works like this, breathe in whilst counting to 4, hold your breath whilst counting to 4 and then breathe out whilst counting to 4, repeat until you feel a sense of calm.

As with every journey, you can't really appreciate it until you have been on it, and it's important to stop and smell the roses whenever you can.

The Rubber Band Model

From 'The Decision Book' Mikel Krogerus and Roman Tschappeler.

Have you ever felt like you were being pulled in two directions when making important decisions? This is a dilemma I have often faced and is common with my clients. We are either wanting to move away from something or towards something; establishing what those forces are is a good place to start.

The rubber band model is a simple way of combining two factors that are at play to help to make the best decision for you. Imagine yourself with a rubber band attached to your current situation and a rubber band attached to your future; each time you pull in one direction, you can feel the tug of the other.

You may have gone through an internal process like this when starting your business, and it would have been a combination of away from and towards factors that led to your decision. When we strike out on our own, we gain freedom but lose a sense of belonging; for instance, the strongest force will win out in the end.

We are motivated by three aspects of our life, what we have experienced up until now, our present circumstances, and our future aspirations. As time goes by, those three aspects change, and so do our motivations, which is important to remember because what's important to us will change.

By spending a bit of time considering the forces that are holding you back and those that are pulling you forward, you can pre-empt the obstacles that may appear.

What's holding you?   What's pulling you?

If you have to decide between two good options, ask
yourself what is holding you and what is pulling you?

"adapted from an image from The Decision Book by M Krogerus & R Tschappeler"

The Obstacle is the way

As Marcus Aurelius put it nearly 2000 years ago: "*The impediment to action advances action. What stands in the way becomes the way.*"

Identifying our biggest obstacle is often where we need to focus our attention rather than trying to avoid it by doing what's easiest. Our own obstacles will be those things that we don't really want to do but are essential for the success of the business.

My obstacle is that I don't really want to be in charge of others, it's something I'm quite capable of doing, and some say I'm good at, but it's not something that I gain energy from. So, for me, my biggest opportunities could well be when I step up and take charge and not shy away from something I regard as futile.

What do you think your biggest obstacle is? It could be tasks that you regard as mundane even though they are vital to the business, or maybe money isn't something you strive for, and consequently, the cash flow in the business is always tight.

I've split this book up into three parts, you, your business, and your team, for the main reason to make you realise you are not your business and you have responsibilities to it as well as your team. It can be difficult to act in the interest of three parties at the same time so you may want to consider getting some accountability set up, which is where a business coach or mastermind group can be useful.

If you think about your motives to start your business, are they the motives that drive you to always do what's right for the business? This is often an important realisation when I discuss this with my clients, which prompts them to either devote time to it or outsource the activities.

When we were working towards our Investors in People accreditation, we did some work around what motivates us, and that is where being in a position of influence came out as my least important. Although I was questioned on how it was going to affect my role as we progressed, it wasn't something I paid much attention to.

Years later, when I ended up spending most of my time doing what didn't motivate me, I realised how important it is to make conscious decisions about what role you really want in your business. We can operate at a high level doing things that don't motivate us for a short time; it's when it becomes long term that the effects of the situation become a problem.

If there's a role in your business that you can do but don't really want to, make it a priority to delegate as soon as possible. We will look at how to create a business and role that's right for you and how to approach recruiting the right people later on in the book.

Develop the skills before you need them

Most of us don't learn to drive when we need to be able to; we learn as soon as possible because we see it as an essential skill that will help us get on in life. In the same vein, it's good to think about the sort of skills you will need as your business grows.

The first skill I encourage you to learn is how to speak in public which is apparently scarier than death for some. I know the first time I put myself forward to speak at a conference my knees were knocking, and my heart was racing.

I had to read a pre-written script whilst changing slides at the same time. As you can probably imagine, the slides didn't always match what I was saying. After it was over, I reflected on how it had gone and received some encouraging feedback which made me feel it was worthwhile.

A few hours later I was in the hotel lift and someone joined from another floor, he turned to me and said, "You were really nervous on the stage this morning". I replied with "Yes, I was". After he left, I thought about what I should have said, which was, "Yes, I was, but sometimes you need to step up and try something scary, and now I've done it."

You are unlikely to bring the house down on your first attempt, but I encourage you to give it a go by starting with a familiar crowd and then building from there. I never hesitate to put myself forward now because I know that each time I do, I learn and get a little bit better.

Another skill I encourage you to spend time understanding is the role of Marketing as, in the words of Peter Drucker, "*There are only two things in a business that make money – innovation and marketing, everything else is cost.*"

In her book 'Watertight Marketing', Bryony Thomas explains how you can develop a marketing process in any business by understanding the buying process and then creating strategies that fix what she calls your leaks.

If you are to create a business and not just a self-employed role, then marketing will be the key to differentiating you from your competition. It will also help you to speak directly to your ideal client, those people you really want to help.

You may not be at a position in your business where marketing is important because you have a good client base, and referrals are coming in regularly. If you have a plan and a system you can switch on when those leads and referrals dry up, then you're in a much better position than if you suddenly had to up your game.

Quite often I see business owners neglecting the role of marketing because they don't understand it, or they see it as self-promotion, which feels uncomfortable. If we are not motivated to promote ourselves, we are unlikely to do it well or even at all, don't leave marketing to chance.

Don't forget those who matter most

I know from experience how your business can take over your life and become all-encompassing. The financial pressure of keeping the business running, the pressure of earning enough to pay the bills and all the other 'must have' things.

It's easy to think that the business is the most important element in your life because without it, everything else will fall apart. I'm not suggesting you should take your eye off the ball, but maybe you need to check in with how you are prioritising your time and energy.

The subject of energy, as I mentioned in the introduction, will come up a lot in this book because we need to manage it and also maximise it. We only have a certain capacity each day to distribute across all the things we need to do, so we need to pay attention to what's most important.

A cautionary tale from my own failing when balancing what's important was back in the days when I was running my retail business. It was my responsibility on a particular day to pick up my daughter from school. It was in my phone to remind me, and as it was just a few minutes away, it wasn't going to take much time.

A short while before I was due to collect her a delivery arrived that needed seeing to and, as you've probably guessed, I forgot to pick her up. Fortunately, my sister in law was picking up my nephew and was waiting with my daughter and eventually realised I was not going to be there, so dropped my daughter off herself.

I can't remember how many times I was reminded of the incident and how long it went on for, but it was a long time. Of course, I was devastated by what had happened, and it was a wake-up call to make sure It didn't happen again.

In 2011, Bronnie Ware, an Australian nurse, wrote a book called 'The Top Five Regrets of the Dying.'

The top five regrets of the dying are:-

I wish I had the courage to live a life true to myself
I wish I hadn't worked so hard
I wish I had the courage to express my feelings
I wish I had stayed in touch with my friends
I wish I had let myself be happier

Make sure you are not missing out on the important things because of the pressures of running the business. Although those pressures are genuine, I know that we can also put unnecessary pressures on ourselves by becoming task-focused and neglecting what's really important.

You don't want to end up one day with a business and maybe a healthy bank balance if all has gone well, with nobody to share it with and lots of regrets from missing out on many of life's true pleasures.

Be careful who you hang out with, avoid isolation.

It can be a lonely place running a business, especially if your friends aren't business owners and they don't really get it. Having a sounding board for your challenges and ideas is an important feedback mechanism that we take for granted when we have a job.

It's also vital that you have the support of your nearest and dearest, make sure they know how important their support is to you. Be aware that they may have their own agenda which doesn't want you to succeed, this can often be due to fear of losing you.

I've had a couple of occasions where I discovered that someone who should have been on my side was working against me in the background. I hope this doesn't happen to you, but I wanted to mention it to serve as a warning that these things can happen.

I have worked with many entrepreneurs who aren't motivated by connecting and community, which was one of the reasons to start their own business. After working on their own, they started to miss the lack of contact with people. I'm writing this book after a year of lockdowns due to the coronavirus pandemic, which has also made people miss that connection.

You may not have thought of it like this, but those conversations can be like a secret board of directors that are advising you without them realising it. As they are really valuable conversations, how can we recreate this scenario?

You may have noticed that co-working spaces are popping up in all sorts of places to cater for solo entrepreneurs and expanding businesses. They offer facilities like high-speed internet, coffee making facilities, and even studios to rent to record videos and podcasts and are great places to get work done.

When you're tired of the same environment and want to meet like-minded business owners, co-working spaces can be ideal. If you make a point of visiting regularly, you will get opportunities to speak with all sorts of people running different businesses in the same way you may have done when employed.

Social media can also be used in a similar way, particularly LinkedIn. By following, connecting, commenting, and posting, you can create your own network of advisors where you can share information. By asking questions in a post, you can get valuable information that will help you before you need to put your hand in your pocket.

Isolation in any situation needs to be avoided, and when running a business, we need to avoid getting stuck in our own heads. How are you going to create your own secret board of advisors who will support you on your journey?

It's how you feel that counts

Are you checking in with how you are feeling? How you feel will have an impact on what you do next, positive or negative, so it's a good idea to be aware. By checking in with ourselves, we can connect with what's important to us.

We tend to blame outside influences for how we are feeling. Take the weather for example; we know a bit of sunshine brightens the day and makes us feel better, even though nothing else in our lives has changed.

When we are feeling good, we are more likely to make better decisions as we are in a better mood or state. Learning how to control our state can have a dramatic effect on what we achieve in life and business. Sometimes the best thing to do is to down tools and go and do something we enjoy, get out in the fresh air and have a bit of fun.

NLP or Neuro-Linguistic Programming is a set of tools and techniques that can also help us control our state by becoming aware of our thinking (Neuro), our Language (Linguistic) and what we do (programming). In her book 'Change Your Life with NLP', Lindsey Agness describes the various ways we can use NLP to create better outcomes.

Every day we are bombarded with information that could easily overwhelm us if there wasn't a system to filter it. We all have filters specific to us that allow us to act on the information we see as relevant to us. This is why we can experience the same event as someone else, but their recollection of it could be totally different to ours.

Once those filters have done their work, we then make an internal representation using our thoughts, which leads to our state of thinking, which leads to a behaviour. With this in mind, we need to be able to control our filters by being focused on what we really want.

You've probably experienced the phenomenon of seeing more of what you're focusing on; typically this happens when we are thinking about purchasing something like a car. What happens is that we have switched our filters to pay particular attention to that type of car, and subsequently we see it everywhere.

When we set out to achieve a goal, we can use this filtering system to help us bring into our lives what we really want. The trick is to be as explicit as possible with our language so we send the right message to our filtering system. This is why we must set goals about what we want and not what we don't otherwise it confuses our filters and can lead us to get more of what we don't want!

You may be thinking, what happens to all this information we receive? We are subconsciously deleting, generalising, and distorting using our own filters before it reaches our brain. This is why we can read a passage of writing that has had all the vowels removed and still make sense of it or miss a repeated word when scanning a document.

How we feel can be affected by the actions of others that led to us feeling a particular way, just one comment can change everything. We always have a choice of whether we allow it to ruin our day. It's worth remembering that a comment is only someone else putting their own filters on the situation.

Learning how to manage our mind and the chatter that's going on is essential for our well-being and the way we feel. I've shared with you my 4:4:4 technique which, when repeated, will slow down your thinking due to the focus on breathing.

To take the breathing exercise a bit further, you may want to consider a mindfulness exercise using meditation. In his book 'The Mindfulness Book' Martyn Newman explains the benefits of meditation, how it works and how to introduce it into your day to day activities.

Martyn shares the four applications of mindfulness, being aware of our thoughts and feelings, checking in with our body, increasing our emotional intelligence and the link to happiness.

By relaxing the body, stabilising the breathing, and focusing the mind, you can achieve more focus and peace in your life. There are also apps you can download to your phone that offer a guided meditation, Headspace and Calm are two I've used.

Be thankful for what you already have

It's easy to fall into the trap of focusing on what we don't have or what has gone wrong and forgetting to appreciate what we have and what has gone well. It's also important to avoid comparing ourselves with others, especially on social media where we only tend to see the upside of most people's lives.

Creating a gratitude journal is one way to promote a feeling of achievement; make it part of your daily habits to look for things to be thankful for by purposefully filling your gratitude bucket.

Don't forget things we take for granted, like the water that comes out of the tap, not everyone in the world has that luxury, or your loving and supporting family.

Don't forget to acknowledge what you have contributed each day, those small acts of kindness that make other people's lives better, like making a cup of tea. They all make a difference and give us purpose.

Being grateful is another way of being mindful by focusing on the moment instead of getting wrapped up in the future. "*There are only two ways to live your life. One is as though nothing is a miracle. The other is as though everything is a miracle*" Albert Einstein.

<u>Summary</u>
Enjoy the journey
The Rubber band model
The Obstacle is the way
Develop skills before you need them
Don't forget what matters most
Be careful who you hang out with, avoid isolation

It's how you feel that counts

Be thankful for what you already have

For extra resources visit **www.motivatedthebook.com**

CHAPTER 2:

Fit Your Own Mask First!

Introduction

If you've flown on an aircraft, you will be familiar with being told in the pre-flight safety briefing that you should fit your own oxygen mask before helping others. There's a good reason why we need to be told this when we are responsible for others, we can easily forget what we need to be in the best position to help those around us.

As a business owner /entrepreneur, it's easy to get wrapped up in the responsibility and, not forgetting, the excitement of running your business. The theme in this chapter is to make sure you are taking care of yourself so you can be the best you can be.

Switching off and Sleep

In her book '24/6 The Power of Unplugging One Day A Week' award-winning film-maker Tiffany Shlain describes how her family decided to go tech-free for one day per week, which she calls their "Technology Shabbat."

Do you remember the days when a mobile phone was just that, a phone to use when we were out and about? Today's smartphones are an important part of our day to day lives and allow us to work on the move, but we need to be mindful with their use.

Tiffany decided to introduce a day free of screen time to reconnect with her family just like it used to be in many cultures on a Saturday or Sunday. She documents the many benefits they gained and also the many challenges they had with sticking to their plan.

Screen time has become a common term in today's world, so much so that we can choose to get a total of that time sent to us each week. This is useful in that what gets measured can be managed. Are you managing your screen time?

One of the things I insisted on when I was running my retail business was a day off each week, and the same went for my team. Getting time away from the business to switch off is essential for your well-being, we are not designed to be constantly on the go.

Our productivity is not dependent on the amount of time we spend on an activity, it's dependent on the quality of the time we spend on it. A 2014 study from Stanford University on 'The Productivity of Working Hours' showed that productivity actually decreased when working over fifty hours a week.

We need to be conscious about the time we are working and ensure we are switching off to recharge, which brings me on to the importance of sleep.

The short term and long term consequences of poor sleep are becoming more and more apparent. Short term consequences are a shorter attention span and a poorer decision-making ability. Long term, they can be cardiovascular disease, diabetes, and cancer.

Whilst writing her book 'The Business of Sleep' Vicki Culpin spent many years looking into the causes, the solutions, and the business case for prioritising sleep. The recommended amount of sleep an adult needs is 8 hours with a variance of between 6 and 10 hours; how many are you getting?

Burning the candle at both ends on a regular basis and relying on caffeine to keep you going through the day is not a good idea. Once you understand the process the brain goes through when we are asleep, you will soon realise you need to prioritise it.

How many times have you had to make an important decision, and when you decided to sleep on it, you woke up with the solution? The quality of our decision-making ability when we are awake is also enhanced when we have had a good night's sleep.

If you are struggling to get the amount of sleep you need, don't be tempted to reach for sleeping pills unless you have been advised to take them. Things you may want to consider are your sleeping environment, having a regular bedtime and regulating your alcohol and caffeine intake.

Food and Exercise

If you want to perform at your best, you need to be aware of what you're putting into your body to refuel. In their book 'How to Have the Energy', Graham Alcott and Colette Heneghan explain how every food choice we make can lead to either brain fuel or potential brain fog.

Your most precious resource is your attention; by picking the right food, you will increase your productivity by increasing your pro-active attention. This is the time when we are fully alert and functioning at our best.

By making better food choices, we are choosing to feel better; one of the biggest challenges is breaking old habits. Those habits start at the point of purchase in the supermarket; Graham and Colette's advice is to avoid foods that have strong branding and their own jingle.

To maximise the energy we get from our food, we need to focus on eating the plant rainbow, not just our greens, eat protein with each meal and be smart with our choice of carbohydrates.

I don't know about you but snacking is my biggest weakness. To stop us reaching for biscuits, chocolate, and crisps, we need to have healthier snacks readily available. The easier you make healthy eating, the more likely you are to stick to it, so make the healthier options easy to find and hide away the unhealthy.

After reading their book, I decided to replace my morning toast or crumpets with overnight oats, which is porridge oats soaked overnight in milk or water. I also replaced fast fermented bread that's made in a factory for locally baked slow fermented sourdough.

These two changes to my diet have given me much more energy, no cravings for snacks or chocolate and increased my attention span. I thought porridge was too much hassle to cook, and then the washing up; I now make it the day before, which takes five minutes and pop it in the fridge. There's lots been written about marginal gains being the difference between winning and losing. What small change to your diet can you make to boost your energy?

It's also important to stay hydrated to maintain mental performance as over 70% of our brain is water; drinking water and limiting the consumption of caffeine is the best option. Always have water available, it's recommended we should drink 1.5 – 2 litres per day, if your wee is more like beer than white wine, that is an indication you may need to drink more water.

At the end of the day, we are human beings not robots, so there will be times when we fall off the wagon. Don't beat yourself up and tell yourself you can't do it; focus on what you have achieved.

We all know we should exercise but sometimes it's the last thing on our minds, especially when we've had a busy day. Dragging yourself out for a run or a gym session when you'd rather sit on the sofa is a big challenge.

Adding exercise into your daily routine doesn't have to mean suddenly introducing a rigorous activity, it's probably not going to be good for you either. When I started to become aware that I needed to start moving a bit more, I made small adjustments to how I did things.

Taking the stairs instead of lifts and walking to the shops not jumping in the car every time is a move in the right direction. I think of this as combining two activities that I need to do at the same time, it's like using my time twice.

One activity I've got into that really works for me is HIIT, High-Intensity Interval Training. It's short bursts of activity followed by a period of rest that lasts for less than an hour. Although it's exhausting, and I feel it in my muscles for a couple of days after, it gives me a positive feeling with the release of endorphins.

What I also use during the sessions is a heart rate monitor that works with an app to give me points for each session. Having that extra bit of feedback and accumulating points towards a monthly goal keeps me going back for more.

Nutrition and Exercise are all about introducing and sticking to healthy habits that will help you feel your best, which in turn will keep you on track, especially when the going gets tough.

Introducing new habits

One of the challenges we all face is introducing new habits that we know are right, but how do we stick to them? In her book 'Better Than Before', Gretchen Rubin suggests it's how we respond to expectations.

There are two types of expectations, outer expectations which are imposed on us by others, and inner expectations we set for ourselves. Our ability to introduce new habits is dependent on how we react to both of these expectations.

I mentioned that I track and receive points for my physical activity using an app and heart monitor; this indicates that I respond to outer expectations that are set for me. I'm also a rule follower, my dad on the other hand was a rule breaker and didn't like to stick to rules and regulations.

What can be useful is to identify how you respond best. Do you need outer expectations, or are you better at setting and responding to your own expectations? How successful have you been in changing your habits in the past? When successful, what were the circumstances? When you failed, what were the circumstances?

Another great book on habit change is 'Atomic Habits' by James Clear, where he talks about the four laws of behaviour change. When planning to introduce a change of habits, the four laws you should bear in mind are, make them obvious, easy, attractive, and satisfying.

When writing this book, I had to introduce new habits to make sure I reached my target and got the book finished and ready for publication. The first thing I did was join a book writing programme that set out the necessary steps and kept me accountable.

Although I wouldn't say the writing was easy, what made it easier was having a book plan with all the chapters and content mapped out before I started writing. This broke down the writing into small chunks which I could write in any order I fancied rather than chronological steps.

The process was attractive because I could see the progress I was making, much like the points I get from my HIIT sessions at the gym. The satisfaction came from posting my progress in the book-writing group and tracking my word count each week.

When I wasn't feeling like writing but knew I had to move the needle, I would stop myself from having my morning coffee until I had completed the required word count. You may have realised that this is one of the last topics I'm writing about, yet it comes quite early on in the book; it is a topic I realised I hadn't included initially but needed to add.

It's all just feedback

This seems like a good point to talk about the importance of giving and receiving feedback. Feedback is a way of communicating that should involve a transfer of value; I say should, because all too often it doesn't feel like that.

I'm sure you have been on the receiving end of some feedback that was not welcome and just felt like it was criticism. What it feels like is important when it comes to delivering good quality constructive feedback.

Feedback is a mechanism to help us judge how we are doing and enables us to stop, start, do more, or do less of something. That is why we need it to be able to grow and make better and more informed decisions. When given well, feedback is a gift.

A pat on the back is a form of feedback that seems to indicate something went well but doesn't actually tell us what we did well. If we don't know what it was, then we can't make a conscious decision around doing more of it in the future.

In her book 'The Feedback Book' Dawn Sillett describes a 4 step process to follow that will deliver clear and actionable feedback. The E.D.G.E framework stands for Explain, Describe, Give and End Positively.

Explain using a clear example of the exact behaviour or action that has prompted your feedback. The sooner, the better, stick to the facts and keep it brief

Describe the effect of the behaviour. What impact has it had? Keep it factual, short, and simple.

Give the recipient the mic. Invite them to speak and give them a fair hearing in their own words. If the feedback is positive, it's their chance to take some credit. If the feedback is about an improvement that's required, this is their chance to take responsibility.

End positively with your encouragement and your recipient's commitment.

I will be revisiting feedback in part three of this book, Motivated Team, as it's something we need to be doing more of especially catching people doing things right.

I want to encourage you to seek feedback whenever the opportunity arises; the more you know and understand about yourself, the better you will be able to adapt to different situations.

In the next chapter, I will introduce a model that helps to explain different behavioural styles and identify what really drives you. There are others that identify strengths and our preferred role in a team and are well worth taking.

When you receive some feedback, check-in with the feeling that comes up and avoid the temptation to refute it. Give yourself time to reflect on the comments and who it came from, and then decide if you need to take any action. If you need a bit more context, a good question to ask is, "that's interesting; tell me more?"

Johari Window

A useful model to demonstrate how giving and receiving feedback can help us was developed by American psychologists Joe Luft and Harry Ingram, which they called the "Johari Window".

Based on what we know about ourselves and what others know about us, we can expand our window of self-awareness using all sorts of feedback mechanisms. We can also share more about ourselves so others understand us, which is particularly useful in team development.

Our Johari Window is split into four panes; the first segment is the Public pane which is what we know about ourselves and is also known to others. This is where we are sharing things about ourselves, such as our likes and dislikes so others understand where we are coming from.

The second pane is the Private pane; this is where we are keeping things that we feel are personal to us or that we feel are best not shared, like a dislike for certain parts of our role.

The third pane is the Blind pane; this is where we can learn from others because it's information that others know about us that we are not aware of. Others may notice that we behave in a particular way when a subject is raised and may then make assumptions about why.

The final pane is the Unknown pane; this pane is about things we have yet to experience that we can therefore only guess our reactions. As we experience life, you could expect this pane to decrease, but that will depend on whether you are seeking out new experiences and feedback.

Seeking feedback and being more open with others will increase the public pane and, at the same time, reduce the private and blind panes. Getting the balance right is important because we don't want to be over sharing inappropriately, and we also don't want to be overly guarded and appear too cagey.

A simple exercise to get feedback is to send a list of values to your trusted network and ask them to pick out four or five that they particularly associate with you. When you receive the responses, ask yourself, are they the values you were expecting or want to see? Are there responses that you thought were obviously your values that nobody chose?

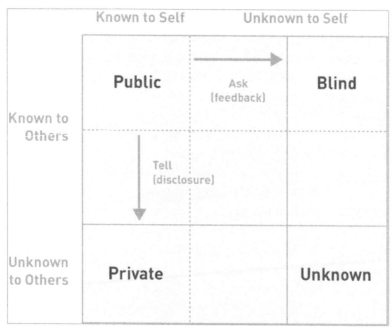

	Known to Self	Unknown to Self
Known to Others	Public → Ask (feedback) ↓ Tell (disclosure)	Blind
Unknown to Others	Private	Unknown

"From Pioneering Professional, D Biddle & A Stewart"

Mindset

As we have considered the importance of feedback, we should remember how feedback makes us feel and the possible consequences. How we process feedback has a big influence on our long term success, both positive and negative.

In her book 'Mindset' Carol Dweck explains the difference between having a Fixed Mindset and a Growth Mindset which is determined by our core beliefs. Having a fixed mindset leads to a belief that we are born with certain abilities, and if we fail it's confirmation we can't do something. A growth mindset considers failure as part of how we learn.

I can remember starting to learn to play various musical instruments and giving up when I didn't get the hang of it as quickly as I thought I should. A growth mindset is essential in business as everything is unlikely to go well the first time we try it, and if we stop giving things a go through the fear of failure, we will never meet our full potential.

Receiving too much of either negative or positive feedback can lead to a fixed mindset as both are confirmation that we are either good or bad at something. Since I embraced the growth mindset, I have given more things a go and guess what, some things, it turns out, I'm quite good at.

Dweck suggests when facing something we've never done before, we should use the word 'yet" I can't speak Spanish yet; I've not bought my dream car yet, it's a clever way of verbalising that you're working toward something but not achieved it yet.

Focus on your strengths

We all have natural strengths that we can easily take for granted, which have helped get us to where we are in life. If we are to lead a life with meaning and purpose, we need to focus and develop our character so we are better equipped for the challenges ahead.

By combining what you believe in with your natural character strengths, you will develop a clear purpose that leads to a more meaningful life. If we choose to be the best versions of ourselves, we need to put into context what that means and what we need to be to achieve it.

There's a saying that we are a combination of the five people we spend the most time with, not forgetting the time we spend with ourselves. With this in mind, we need to be mindful of the influences we are surrounding ourselves with and make active choices in that regard.

In their book 'Character Strengths and Virtues' Christopher Peterson and Martin Seligman identify 24 character strengths that are pivotal in becoming the best versions of ourselves. By identifying our strengths and also our perceived weaknesses, we can focus our attention where it's needed most.

The 24 Character Strengths identified are:

Character Strengths

Creativity	Curiosity	Love of Learning	Perspective	Bravery	Gratitude
Perseverance	Honesty	Enthusiasm	Love	Kindness	Optimism
Social Intelligence	Social Responsibility	Teamwork	Fairness	Leadership	Humour
Forgiveness	Humility	Prudence	Self-Control	Appreciation of Beauty	Spirituality

What are your strengths, and how do you use them each day? Which ones, if you focused on them, would make the biggest difference in your life and business? Which ones do you see in the five people that you spend the most time with?

Why not send these character traits to your circle of influence and ask them what they think are your strengths and do the same for them in return? By focusing on our strengths and pointing out the strengths of others, you are promoting a feeling of positivity.

Embrace your story

You may have noticed that I share parts of my story as I cover the topics in this book, and hopefully, this will help you understand why it's important. Emotional connection is an integral part of selling and marketing, and there are not many things more emotive than our own story.

When my father started our family retail business, he did so because he wanted to escape the corporate world, do something for himself and create a legacy that my brothers and I could carry on. That is essentially what happened. As time went by, we took over the running of the business, and he left to pursue other business interests.

We lived and breathed that story for many years, our customers related to the story, and it became part of our brand. Looking back, a mistake we made when my father left the business was not redefining our vision based on the continuation of the story.

We were still successful in growing the business, but I believe we would have been even more successful if we had used our story more to connect at an emotional level to our customers in our marketing. I'll cover how important motivation is in our work in later chapters, it's also important when it comes to buying decisions.

In 2009 the UK government produced a report, which came to be known as the Macleod report, which sought to consolidate best practice in enabling employee engagement. According to the report, there are four major enablers of employee engagement, one of which is particularly associated with having a strong, strategic narrative (story).

The story allows customers and employees alike to connect to the why of the business; without it they are left to make up their own minds. We are lucky that we have choices as to where we work and where we spend our money, and many of those decisions are based more on emotion than logic.

If you feel good about where you work and where you spend your money, you will likely build up a sense of loyalty. When I created the Reluctant Leader Academy, it was based on my own story and my vision of preventing others from making the same mistakes as I did, so contributing to my clients' future story.

I hope you can see the value of connecting to your story and why it makes good sense for your internal and external marketing. Next time you happen to be watching the adverts on TV, notice how stories are being used to connect you on an emotional level to the product or service.

Never Stop Learning

As you are reading this book, hopefully, you have made reading part of your self-development plan. One of the character traits that's most associated with achievement, success and happiness is curiosity.

Remaining curious and constantly questioning the status quo keeps us open-minded and helps us to adapt to the rapidly changing world. Whether you prefer to read books, listen to podcasts or watch YouTube videos, developing a love of learning is essential.

Being curious will keep your thinking fresh and allows you to flexible when faced with challenges you've never faced before. Curiosity is about asking questions like "how can we do this better or fast?' to a wide range of people that will have a different view of the situation.

I used to love reading autobiographies of sports personalities and famous celebrities; how they became successful fascinated me. Nowadays, I read more on self-development. Read, watch or listen to whatever inspires you to improve and take responsibility for your own development and success.

Summary
Switching off and sleeping
Nutrition and Exercise
It's all just feedback
Johari window
Mindset
Focus on your strengths
Embrace your story
Never stop learning

For extra resources visit **www.motivatedthebook.com**

Mirror

CHAPTER 3:

Mirror – Self Awareness is Key

Introduction

As a business owner or entrepreneur, it's easy to be focused on getting things done, forgetting the impact we have on those around us, particularly our team. One thing is for certain, everything you do and how you do it is being noticed. For this reason, you need to be aware of the impact you are having on those around you.

In this chapter, we are going to look at ways you can hold up the mirror and get the critical knowledge that will set you apart from most business owners. Once you are aware of your own strengths and weaknesses, you will be in a much better position to understand others.

To be more successful, you need to realise that operating independently will not create the best environment for success. We need to develop a culture of interdependency by taking responsibility, being proactive and working with others. This is why Mirror is the first important element of getting the M.E.A.S.U.R.E. of your business.

Behavioural Styles

When we understand others, we can better appreciate the value that they bring, "*If one does not understand a person, one tends to regard him as a fool*" Dr Carl G Jung

You have undoubtedly come across people you regard as challenging because they do things differently to you. The danger is that we see our way as right and their way as wrong which can lead to misunderstanding and conflict.

We can only picture the world as we see it based on what we have experienced and how we have been successful in the past. We are unlikely to want to change something that we understand for something untested unless we can be sure it will work, so we stick to what we know.

Appreciating each other's strengths is where we should start, which goes against what we have probably experienced ourselves. How many times have you been told that you've got something wrong, compared to how many times you have been praised for getting something right?

If we are going to become interdependent and work with others effectively, then we need to see the good in others and not focus on their faults. Having Positive Regard and the ability to get on with others is an essential part of being an effective business owner.

Dr Carl G Jung published his book, 'Psychological Types' in 1923 based on his research, it has been widely used in the creation of Psychometric tests to establish behavioural styles. It's been established that there are four types of behaviour which we all have but in different proportions which make us unique.

Our mix of these four types will determine how we respond to the challenges we face and how we interact with others. There are a number of ways that these behavioural styles can be represented, by using letters, archetypes and even animals, but I prefer to use colours which I find easy to relate to and remember when it comes to behaviour traits.

What's your colour mix?

Why did he do that? How could they possibly come to that conclusion?

Our perception of any situation is coloured by the person we are. Our own actions are driven by our intentions; others don't see the intentions, just the results and their perception may be totally different.

If you had to choose, which one of these groups of statements feels most like you?

Blue – task-focused and introverted, logical and analytical, enjoys problem-solving, needs time to reflect, realistic, sorts out the details, strong sense of duty, structured and disciplined

Red – task-focused and extroverted, bold and determined, confident and optimistic, enjoys stretching goals, leads from the front, sets a winning mentality, thinks big, direct and to the point

Yellow – people-focused and extroverted, free-spirited, friendly and optimistic, generous and open-minded, inspirational and visionary, looks on the bright side, spontaneous and imaginative

Green – people-focused and introverted, considerate and caring, genuine concern for colleagues, avoids conflict, involves others in decisions, respects others' values, supportive and loyal

Whichever one you choose is most probably the style you lead with, and the other colour energies are second, third and fourth. We are not just one style but a blend of all four, which makes up our colour profile.

We can also adapt our style depending on the situation and, in particular, how we turn up at work. The more we feel we need to adapt our style to meet the situation and environment at work, the more uncomfortable we are likely to feel.

Each of the colours has its strengths and weaknesses

Blue strengths – realistic, detail-focused, logical, clarity to complexity, calm in a crisis
Blue possible weaknesses – emotionally detached, lacks spontaneity, hypercritical
Red strengths – bold, plays to win, decisive, thrives on pressure, makes an impact
Red possible weaknesses – only results matter, short fuse, intolerant, not listening
Yellow strengths – energetic, positive outlook, zest for life, sociable, enthusiastic
Yellow possible weaknesses – miss details, everything to excess, disorganised
Green strengths – tactful, supportive, considerate, peacemaker, tolerant, reliable
Green possible weaknesses – lacks urgency, indecisive, lacks conviction, self-critical

If we are going to lead a business effectively, we need to use all four colour energies at the appropriate times, we will look at this in more detail in part three of the book.

www.colour-profiling.com

What gets you out of bed?

When I start working with my clients, there are some tell-tale signs that they aren't feeling great about their business. It could be their body language, the words they use or the classic dropping of the shoulders when they are talking about their business.

The question I use most often is, "How easy is it to get out of bed in the morning? If 10 is I can't wait to get to work and 1, is I delay it as long as possible, where are you?" This tends to lead to a discussion around different days being easier than others, and we start to pull out the differences between a good day and a bad day.

Wherever you are on your business journey, it's important to check in with how you are feeling about your business or, in other words, how motivated you are. Motivation is the motive, the internal reason, to act in a certain way and is driven from within us.

When we are motivated, we are full of this invisible energy that makes us feel good and drives us forward if we are to make the most of this energy, we need to create the right conditions to allow it to flow.

You may, at this point, be thinking what about motivational speakers? If you have listened to someone who describes themselves as a motivational speaker, you will have probably noticed that they tell a story. The story tends to be one that describes a journey from adversity through to overcoming that adversity, which I will suggest is more inspirational than motivational.

A useful analogy when referring to motivation in a business context is the fuel that gets you going and keeps you going. To continue the vehicle analogy, your business journey is dependent on setting a direction (steering wheel), deciding on how you will get there (vehicle) and a purpose for keeping going (fuel).

We know what will happen if our vehicle runs out of fuel, it will gradually start to slow down and eventually stop altogether. This is why we need to keep topping up our fuel by feeding whatever it is that gives us energy at work and fulfilling our motivators is how we do this.

Our motivations, unlike behavioural styles, are quite likely to change so we need to be able to check-in with what is motivating us from time to time. You may have set up your business because you wanted more recognition for your expertise, but as time has gone by freedom has become more important.

James Sale, the creator of Motivational Maps, explains in his book 'Mapping Motivation' the reason our motivations change is due to three primary sources of motivation, our personality based on our past, our self-concept based on what's going on in our lives right now, and our future expectations based on what we want in the future.

These three elements are changeable, particularly the latter two, so we need to check in with our motivations with a view to maintaining and improving our motivation levels as our needs and wants change.

What we need to learn is how to feed our motivators by seeking the appropriate rewards, and to do this, we need a way to identify, measure and describe motivation.

Motivational maps – a language to describe motivation

If I ask someone what motivates them about their work, they typically mention things like, "It lets me buy the nice things in life", "it gives me three great holidays per year", or "It helps me pay the mortgage off". These are all worthy reasons, but as a business owner, we need to be more in tune with what is really driving those desires.

Motivational Maps is an online diagnostic tool created by James Sale in 2005 that allows us to tap into those inner drivers that are important to us. Like the four different behavioural styles, in this case there are nine motivators that we all have within us.

By identifying the strength of each motivator, the diagnostic can then put them in the order of importance from most important down to least important. We also get a fulfilment level for each of the motivators, which indicates how we are feeling about how each is currently being met.

Although we need to be aware of all nine, the initial focus is on the top three and also the bottom or least important motivator. As a business owner, it's easy to end up neglecting our top motivators and spend too much time on things associated with our lowest, which in motivational terms is a double whammy.

The nine motivators are grouped into three clusters of three: a relationship cluster, an achievement cluster, and a growth cluster. By identifying which is the strongest cluster, we can get a feel for where we are focusing our attention, either towards nurturing relationships, a desire for achievement or for our personal development or growth.

The three relationship motivators are

The Defender – seeks security, predictability, stability
The Friend – seeks belonging, friendship, fulfilling relationships
The Star – seeks recognition, respect, social esteem

The three achievement motivators are

The Director – seeks power, influence, control of people/resources
The Builder — seeks money, material satisfactions, above average living standards
The Expert – seeks expertise, mastery, specialisation

The three growth motivators are

The Creator – seeks innovation, identification with new, expressing creative potential
The Spirit – seeks freedom, independence, making own decisions
The Searcher – seeks meaning, making a difference, providing worthwhile things

"From Mapping Motivation by James Sale"

Which of the motivators do you think are most important to you? Try putting them in order of importance, and then think about how each one is being met in your role. This is quite a difficult exercise, and in my experience, when comparing their choices with the result from the online diagnostic, most don't really know their key drivers.

I've had clients recognise that what they thought was their most important motivator ended up being their least important, which turned out to be quite a pivotal moment. One of the reasons this happens is the confusion between needs and wants; we may need more money but what we really want is to do something we see as worthwhile.

We may need more money because we don't think we earn enough, but what we really want is to be recognised for what we do, or to make a difference. There are no right or wrong motivations; what's important is, are those motivations being fulfilled in what we do, and what is missing or could be our potential Achilles heel?

We've looked at behavioural styles, how we do what we do, and Motivation, why we do what we do; let's look at impacts we can have on others.

Your Personal Impact

Our impact is the effect we have on those around us, which can be affected by the way we dress and how we interact with others. We know we are influenced by brands, so if you were a brand, what would be included in your brand guidelines?

The first thing to consider is the way you dress. Think of this as your packaging, and we know how important that is when we are buying products. I had a friend, a financial advisor, who had questionable taste in socks and ties; for some people this could be interpreted as unprofessional.

Have a think about the impression you want to give to your clients, customers, and suppliers. I'm not suggesting you should be dressed up all the time, but we must keep in mind how others may be judging us; we don't want to undermine what we hope to achieve.

If you are unsure about what is appropriate, there are specialist stylists that will help you buy the right things and advise on what to wear for different situations. Make sure if you go down this route that you feel comfortable and ensure that what you are wearing makes you feel good.

It's worth mentioning that you don't have to be perfect. In her book 'The Gifts of Imperfection', Brene Brown writes about the struggles we all have living up to our own expectations. If we live in fear of making a mistake and what people think of us, we are creating unnecessary anxiety.

If you feel your levels of stress and anxiety are growing, then you are probably taking on too much responsibility. I say this from my own experience, taking responsibility away from my team to relieve some stress and inadvertently adding to my own stress levels.

Having the right leadership mindset is essential; let's look at that in a bit more detail.

Your Leadership Attitude

I mentioned in the introduction to this book that I'd never had any leadership training when I was running my retail business. It wasn't until I sold that business and was considering what to do next that I came across a programme that would have been perfect for me.

Dr Derek Biddle and Ali Stewart had been working together for many years, and after testing and refining, they created a programme which they made available for others to use, which they named Liberating Leadership. It was on my first day of training to become accredited to use the programme that I came across the concept of High Challenge and High Support.

Our approach to leading will be dependent on our underlying beliefs and attitude or simply our mindset toward leading and managing others. The way we see things, our lens, will influence our approach, so we need to be consciously aware of our resulting attitude.

In their book, 'Liberating Leadership' Derek and Ali explain the importance of developing the mindset of High Challenge and High Support by showing positive regard and genuineness.

An example of using high challenge and high support would be when you are asked for help to solve a problem. The High Support way would be to give them a solution; the High Challenge way would be to tell them it's their job, and to work it out for themselves. A High Support and High challenge way would be to ask, before giving any assistance, "What would you do if I wasn't here?"

The message you are giving is, I'm here to help, but I know you are able to solve this yourself. There will be times when you need to step in to solve problems quickly due to an urgent situation. What you need to avoid is taking that route too often and thereby creating a team that becomes dependent on you.

There are many concepts that are part of the Liberating Leadership Programme that have had a positive effect on how I approach aspects of life; High Challenge and High Support has been the one that has been the most profound. If you are to create a business that sets you free, I encourage you to embrace the concept.

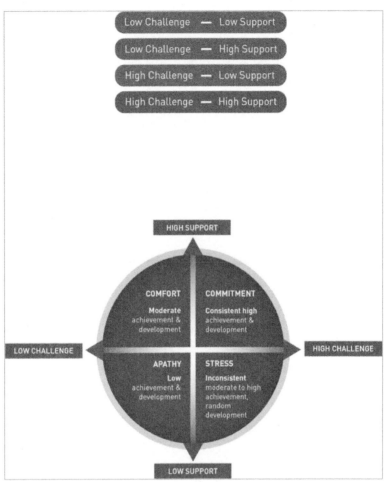

Low Challenge — Low Support

Low Challenge — High Support

High Challenge — Low Support

High Challenge — High Support

HIGH SUPPORT

LOW CHALLENGE

HIGH CHALLENGE

COMFORT
Moderate achievement & development

COMMITMENT
Consistent high achievement & development

APATHY
Low achievement & development

STRESS
Inconsistent moderate to high achievement, random development

LOW SUPPORT

"From Liberating Leadership, D Biddle & A Stewart"

Would you apply for your job, avoiding the swamp?

If you have a job description for all of your team, do you have one for yourself? If your first reaction is general dogsbody, then you definitely need to complete this exercise. As I've mentioned before, it's oh so easy to create a role that's made up of all the tasks nobody else wants to do, and it's unlikely this will keep you motivated.

Let's start with your job title, does it describe your role accurately? If it has 'Managing' in the title, is your main responsibility to manage and are you doing it? Did you intend to become a manager?

A great example of someone who didn't want to be a managing director is James Sale, the creator of "Motivational Maps'. With his insight, he knew that with his high creator motivation and low director motivator, his ideal job title would be Creative Director, so that is what he does, and his wife is Managing Director.

We can all do things well that don't motivate us for a short while, but as time goes by, it becomes a problem and can easily turn into resentment. You may well be good at something you spend a lot of your time doing, but if it doesn't motivate you, eventually it will catch up with you.

If you are happy with your title, what are your day to day responsibilities to the business? In their book "Rocket Fuel", Gino Wickman and Mark C Winters describe the two roles that business owners generally fall into, either Visionary or Integrator.

The Visionary has traits that are entrepreneurial, inspired, passionate, has big ideas, big problem solver, learner, researcher, vision creator. The challenges they have are inconsistency, lack of clear direction, reluctance to let go, no patience for the details and leaves their team behind.

An Integrator has traits that are clarity, communication, focus, accountability, team unity, execution, steady, consistent, follow through. The challenges they have are the job can be thankless, accusations of pessimism, frustration balancing resources, having to do the dirty work and being accused of moving too slowly.

Which role resonates with you the most? If you had the choice, which one would you choose? You may be playing both roles, so this could be a good time to become more of one than the other and then recruit for the other role; one thing is for certain, your business needs both.

When I started to take more responsibility in our retail business, I was definitely the integrator, and my father was the visionary. As time went by, I stepped into the visionary role as my father spent less and less time in the business.

Being clear about your ideal role will prevent you getting caught in the swamp. This is a reference to the boiling frog myth that if you put a live frog in a pan of boiling water, it will immediately jump out to save itself. If, alternatively, you placed the frog in a tepid pan of water and then heated it on the stove, the frog would perish before it realises what is happening and gets boiled to death.

We can easily allow things to creep up on us like the frog and then wonder why we aren't enjoying what we are doing. Be aware of the environment you are creating and don't get caught in the swamp!

Don't be a Grump!

If you are getting your key motivators met, this is hopefully not a problem for you, but it's worth remembering that nobody wants to work for or with a grump. The whole of part one of this book has been devoted to setting you up to be the best you can be and making the most of running your business.

You need to be sharing laughter at work, and sometimes that may mean laughing at yourself. I'm not suggesting you dress up like a clown but seeing the funny side of things when they don't go to plan is good for you and those you work with. Richard Branson is well known for the antics he gets into to promote his businesses; he clearly doesn't take himself too seriously and likes to have fun at work.

A study at the Yale University School of Management found that among working groups, cheerfulness and warmth spread most easily, while irritability is less contagious.

By remaining positive and cheerful, you are helping yourself, and your team stay positive. In their book 'The Art of Possibility', Rosalind and Benjamin Zander introduce Rule number 6, which is "*don't take yourself so g...damn serious*ly". Don't let your demands and feeling of entitlement get the better of you.

<u>Summary</u>
Behavioural Styles
What's your colour mix?
What gets you out of bed in the morning?
Motivational Maps
Your Personal Impact
Your Leadership Mindset
Avoiding the swamp
Don't be a grump!
For extra resources visit **www.motivatedthebook.com**

PART TWO: MOTIVATED BUSINESS

In this part of the book, we are going to look at how to create the business that will set you free, one that doesn't feel like a business at all. We will look at the key elements to consider What you do, how you do it and Why it matters.

We will look at the next three steps in the M.E.A.S.U.R.E system, Evaluate, Action and Systemise.

Evaluate

CHAPTER 4:

Evaluate – Where Are You Now and Where Are You Going?

Introduction

There's a lot of talk about purpose in business, which is a good thing, but is quite often over-complicated; staying connected to the outcome we are creating is what we need to focus on. There are many reasons to start a business; whether it's to make money, make a difference, freedom to make your own choices, all reasons are valid.

The most important thing is to be clear on your reason and then create a business that will fulfil that need. If your business is going to be a Motivated Business, then you need to be clear on what that means to you.

The way you approach this part of the process will be influenced by your current motivations. Are you mainly relationship, achievement, or growth motivated? There's no right or wrong answer, but if you are going to create a business for the long term, you need to focus on what your needs and wants will be long term.

What problem are you solving?

Every business that has ever been started was set up to solve a problem, so we need to be clear as to what that problem is. The three things we need to consider are, what is the problem, how do we want to fix it, and why does it matter?

Let's take supermarkets which, as you know, are something I've spent a lot of my time working in. Is every supermarket set up to solve the same problem? You could say that they are all there to supply the needs of their customers with a range of goods.

When my father set up our family retail business, he had come from many years of doing the same for a national retailer. His experience was supplying a wide range of products at competitive prices to as many people as possible.

After a while, he realised that the problem we were trying to solve in a neighbourhood store was different to the one he had been solving before. Where price used to be an important factor in the large supermarkets, what was now more important was convenience.

Back in the mid-1980s, stores that stayed open seven days a week and early 'til late were few and far between. Our store didn't open on Sundays and we closed at 5:30pm each day, which wasn't particularly convenient.

After a weekend trip to the seaside, not to sit on the beach but to visit so-called convenience stores, we took the decision to open seven days a week from 8 am 'til 8 pm. We were now not going to compete on price but convenience and serve our customers in a new way.

Nowadays we are used to having many stores that are open all day every day to serve our every need. That problem has well and truly been fixed; the challenge for many convenience store operators is which problem now needs to be solved.

When you are clear on the problem you are solving, it makes it a lot easier to take the next step, so let's look at how we can do that.

The Crossroads Model

Wherever you are on your business journey, it's worth stopping and considering the options available and asking some important questions. The Crossroads model from 'The Decision Book' was inspired by the Personal Compass, developed by San Francisco consulting agency The Grove.

The model asks these five questions:

Where have you come from?
What is Really important to you?
Which People are important to you?
What is hindering you?
What are you afraid of?

The way we think about each of these questions will be influenced by our motivations and whether relationships, achievement or growth is our driving force.

Where have you come from is a question based on our past and is associated with the relationships we have had. We are heavily influenced by our parents before we start school, when at school we are influenced by our teachers and when we reach the workplace it's our boss.

The experiences we had, good and bad, will have shaped our view of the world and how we lead our life, what important events have shaped your thinking?

What is really important to you will depend on whether you are focused on relationships, achievements or growth. If relationships are dependent on what has happened to us, achievements are more about what going on right now and growth is about the future and what you want to be.

Which People are important to you is an important question when it comes to achieving your goals. We can achieve things quicker on our own but If we want to achieve more then we need to go with others, choosing the right people essential and remembering those who support us along the way.

What is hindering you can often be associated with where you focus the least amount of your time, or in other words, what least motivates you. It's important to make sure you are maximising the time you spend doing things that motivate you but you should be wary of neglecting important elements of your business because you don't want to do them.

What are you afraid of is an important question in that we are often just as much afraid of success as we are of failure. Is the fear of change or doing something way outside of your comfort zone holding you back?

Businesses are continually moving through development phases and our motivations and communication styles will affect how comfortable we feel at each stage. The Five Elements model is a great way to illustrate those phases or seasons.

"adapted from an image from The Decision Bookby M Krogerus & R Tschappeler"

The Five Elements Model

Part of the Evaluate process is deciding where you want to go, but before you do that, it's a good idea to check where you are so you can measure progress. You then need to decide where you want to go, how you will get there, what resources you need and then put the plan into action.

In their book 'Mapping motivation for Leadership', James Sale and Jane Thomas share a useful process which they call the Five Elements Model and details the steps a business needs to take when establishing their next move. The steps follow a cycle that begins and ends with checking:

Checking – where are we now?
Visioning – where do we want to be?
Planning – how will we get there?
Facilitation – what resource do we need?

Doing – what actions happen?
Checking – what have we achieved

By following this process, you will make sure you are spending appropriate time at each step, which is important to remember. You are probably more interested in and good at some of the steps than others; personally Visioning and Facilitating are my strengths.

When we are in the Visioning and Planning stages, we are in our heads thinking about the future. When we move to the facilitating and doing stages, we will be involving others to make this happen. In Part three of the book, we will look in a bit more detail at how we need to engage our team in our vision and the key skills to get them on board.

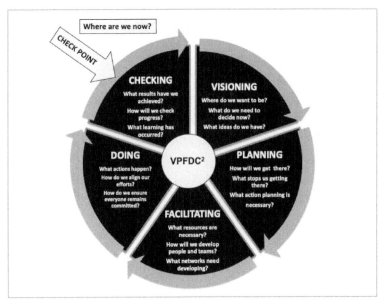

"From Mapping Motivation for Leadership by James Sale & Jane Thomas"

80

The Role of a Coach

By now, you should be aware of your behavioural style, your current motivations and the steps in the five elements model that you're best suited to. Finding the right support to help you make the most of your strengths and avoid your weaknesses tripping you up can be really useful.

A coach is not there to give you the answers; that's more of a mentoring role which is normally someone who has successfully achieved what you're working towards or is a few steps ahead of where you are now. A coach will ask great questions, keep you accountable and support you in achieving your goals.

A coaching relationship needs to have a foundation of trust and be focused on moving forward by taking action. Picking the right coach is about getting the balance of challenge and support right; too much of one without the other is unlikely to lead to success.

If you pick a coach who is very supportive but doesn't challenge you to do the things you know you need to do, then you could end up just having a friendly chat. If you pick a coach that lacks support but continually challenges you, you could make great progress but get stressed out in the process.

I've had several coaches over the years who have helped me through challenging times and when I wanted to make what felt like a leap forward in my business. My top tip would be to take your time and take advantage of any free sessions that are offered without feeling you have to move to a paid engagement until you are ready to do so.

I covered the importance of looking after yourself physically and emotionally in part one, where I stressed the importance of exercise, diet, sleep and switching off. You can find coaches for all these things, and you may decide a coach in these areas would be more beneficial than a business coach. Stephen Covey, in his book 'The Seven habits of highly effective people', says one of the seven habits is *'Put First Things First'*; if you focus on your business and continually sacrifice your wellbeing and your relationships, you may end up with a successful business but at what cost?

You can get a coach for just about anything you want to improve in your life or business; the dilemma is often where to start. I've mentioned the importance of marketing in part one, I'd also recommend getting support when deciding on your branding.

I made the mistake of focusing on sales coaching before I had got clear on the problem I wanted to solve and for whom. If you spend time on getting your marketing and branding really focused on your ideal client, I think you'll find the sales conversations you have with your potential clients will become much easier.

You may have realised that you have a coaching role to play with developing your team. We will cover the importance of coaching when leading your team in part three of this book.

Creating a Motivated Vision

Imagine starting a building project with a piece of land and a pile of bricks without any idea what you wanted to build, and you just start putting brick upon brick.

You would eventually get to a point where you have something you can say looks like a building, but it's unlikely to be ideal.

A vision is what you need before an architect draws a plan; you wouldn't just ask a builder to build a house without giving them a plan. Your vision for your house will be about how you want to live so the architect can bring it to life.

The simplest vision I've heard was the new head of a school in a run-down inner-city area declaring that the vision was to remove the bars from the windows. The bars were obviously there for a reason, so that reason needed to be removed.

Whether the vision actually happened or not, I'm not sure, but from the day it was announced, everyone knew what they were working towards. You may think that if it wasn't successful, then they failed, but a vision isn't dependent on the event happening, it's more important role is to set a direction.

We are all used to people asking, "what do you do for a living?" and the answer is generally around what we do as a job. In the above case, it would have been I'm a headteacher, imagine that headteacher instead saying, "I'm a headteacher, and I'm working to remove the bars from the windows of my school". Isn't that a far more inspiring way to introduce yourself that's more about "the why"?

So, a vision should be inspirational and easy to understand, but we also need to break it down so that we can connect to why it matters to us. As we have already explored, we all have different reasons to get out of bed in the morning, so it's a good idea to connect the vision to that why.

Many businesses are set up around what and how they do what they do. In his book 'Start with Why', Simon Sinek explains the importance of knowing why you do what you do. It can often set you apart from your competition and keep you focused on why what you do and how you do it matters.

How you connect to your vision will depend on a number of elements, mainly your previous experience, your skills, your behavioural style, and your motivations. We need some logic in how we do things but what really keeps us doing what we do is our emotions which are closely linked to our motivations.

What keeps you connected to your business is your 'Why', which is driven by your motivations, so what we need to be aware of is how we feel those motivations are being fulfilled. This is where we need to consider the factors that are important to us that lead us to feel motivated.

Here are the nine motivators again with their associated values

Defender – high job security, clear role & responsibilities
Friend – feel you belong, friendly environment, supported
Star – social recognition, being valued, respected
Director – in charge, decision-maker, responsibility
Builder – good standard of living, winning, success
Expert – opportunities to learn, share expertise, specialist
Creator – change & variety, problem solver, innovation
Spirit – working autonomously, having a choice, flexible
Searcher – meaning & purpose, important work, making a difference

A motivated vision needs to have a What, a How, and a Why and a way of connecting to that vision on a personal level by knowing why it matters to you.

Make it Visual

As you formulate your ideas, it can be useful to make them visual for others to see, and this will also act as a working model. 'The Business Model Canvas' comprises nine sections and asks nine questions about who you serve, how you operate, and the resources you need.

Section one is customer segments. Who are your ideal customers? Who are you creating value for, and who are your most important customers? Are they in a particular industry, a particular size, are they a person or an organisation?

Section two is value proposition. What are the products and services you deliver to your customer segment, what value do you deliver to them, what problem do you solve, and why is it important?

Section three is revenue streams. How do you receive payment for your product or service? This could be a mixture of one-off, regular, short term or long term contracts, licensing or commissions.

Section four is your channels. How do you deliver your value propositions, how do you deliver your product or services to your customers? How will you distribute to your customers? Will it be direct to the consumer or via a partner?

Section five is customer relationships. How do you show up, and how do you attract, sell to and maintain the relationship with your customers?

Section six is key activities. What do you need to do each day to maintain your business model? This could include managing cash flow, marketing, developing new products and services

Section seven is key resources. What people, premises, IT systems, software, products do you need to deliver your value proposition?

Section Eight is key partners. They could be providing advice, funding, collaborations, referrals, transportation, supplies and manufacturing

Section Nine is Cost structure. Fixed costs such as premises, staff, and vehicles to variable costs like fuel, raw materials and marketing

I recommend printing a large format version and placing the completed canvas in a place where you can easily keep it updated and use it to talk any new recruits through how all the elements work together and where their role fits in.

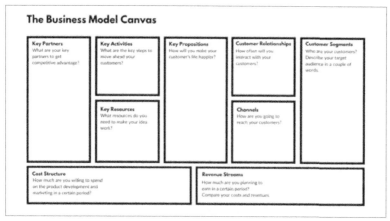

The Business Model Canvas

Key Partners	Key Activities	Key Propositions	Customer Relationships	Customer Segments
What are your key partners to get competitive advantage?	What are the key steps to move ahead your customers?	How will you make your customer's life happier?	How often will you interact with your customers?	Who are your customers? Describe your target audience in a couple of words.
	Key Resources		Channels	
	What resources do you need to make your idea work?		How are you going to reach your customers?	

Cost Structure	Revenue Streams
How much are you willing to spend on the product development and marketing in a certain period?	How much are you planning to earn in a certain period? Compare your costs and revenues.

"www.strategyzer.com/canvas/business-model-canvas"

Track your progress

If you have completed the Business Canvas exercise, you will have a clear idea of all the elements of your business that need to be monitored. A dynamic business will be constantly evolving and adapting to the market conditions and looking for ways to improve.

Setting targets is essential to give you something to aim at and then something to check in the business cycle as described in the Five Elements model. Make them a stretch but be careful not to make them unrealistic. Making them achievable and connected to the wider vision is ideal.

Your business will be dependent on a regular stream of leads and enquiries, so you need to think about how that will be achieved. This is where your marketing fits in, to attract your ideal customer to you by the messaging you put out using whichever channel you feel appropriate.

Where you put out your messaging will depend on where your customer is likely to be hanging out. Social media is one way you may want to reach your customers by creating content that is useful and attracts them to find out more. If you are clear on your value propositions, you should be able to create content that will be well received.

A great book on the subject is 'They Ask You Answer', by Marcus Sheridan, it's about creating content that answers commonly asked questions from your ideal customer. By answering those questions, you are building up trust by sharing your knowledge and expertise, so when the time is right, you will be top of mind.

We are now able to easily research anything we are thinking of buying on the internet, so we are in a much better place to make an informed decision. As previously mentioned, telling a story in our marketing has become an effective way to add value and connect on an emotional level with our customers.

Measuring the effectiveness of your messaging and content is important so you can monitor what is working, this is where technology is essential to capture the data. Measuring things like website visitors, social media followers and how many downloads of free information will give you an idea about how you are doing.

Your revenue streams are essential to keep money flowing through your business, so monitoring when money is due in and due out is vital. It's also important to track your conversion rates from leads, enquiries through to becoming clients.

Measure how you are doing with existing clients, it's important to check in with how you are doing by asking for feedback.

This is another point where you can capture important data that will help you keep improving, and technology can help by collecting the data in one place.

When collecting feedback, make it as easy as possible to complete by creating a set of multiple-choice questions and then sending a link to your client stating how long it takes; ideally this should take less than five minutes.

Peter Drucker, the management guru, once said, '*What gets measured, gets managed*,' so the more you measure, the more you can manage and control in your business.

Who not How

As you know now, as a business owner, it's important to know your strengths, in particular, what you like doing rather than what you're good at. The question to ask is not can I do that, but do I want to do it? A great book on the subject is 'Who not How' by Dan Sullivan with Dr Benjamin Hardy

In their book, Dan and Benjamin tell the story of Michael Jordan needing a Who, not a How and when he did that, he started to truly become the star he was destined to be. If you want your business to grow beyond your capabilities, you need to have the mentality of finding the right people rather than learning new skills.

If your business is going to set you free, you need to avoid the trap of thinking you can learn a new skill, instead of asking the question, "How can I achieve this goal" ask "Who can help me achieve this?". Crucially 'Who' creates Results 'How" creates problems.

If you recruit the right people, they will take the responsibility away from you and will more than likely do a better job and add value to the process. If your vision is clear for all to see and understand, then this should be a natural step for you to take.

If you're not ready to recruit for a role, you can find freelancers for just about anything these days that can fill the gap. You can start with a few hours and then move up to a few days until you get to the point where you need to recruit.

I mentioned in chapter one that you can create a secret board of advisors by networking and connecting with people on social media. When the time is right, that network will be invaluable and should save you money and, most importantly, time.

In 'Mapping motivation for leadership', James Sale and Jane Thomas share the 4 + 1 model. It outlines the four key elements of leadership, Thinking, Doing, Team building and Motivating. The +1 element is Self, looking after yourself and developing yourself is essential, as we have covered in part one of this book.

Making time to think is essential, where you can problem solve and plan. Doing is about overseeing projects, recruiting the right people, and systemising, which we will cover in Chapter six.

Team Building and Motivating your team are the tasks you should not outsource as they are your key responsibility. Learning how to get the most from everyone on your team is the key to creating a business that sets you free which we'll cover in Part Three of this book.

Values not rules

Gone are the days when a staff handbook with all the rules and regulations will cut it when it comes to employee engagement. As Jim Collins wrote in his book 'Good to Great', you've got to get the right people on the bus and the wrong people off the bus, and what defines good people are those who share similar values.
Our values are our deeply held beliefs that have been created by our past experiences, our upbringing, and people we have spent time with. Values give meaning to our lives and guide our decisions and the choices we make. If we are going to create a business that sets us free, we want to attract people that share our values.

Our motivations are closely linked to our values and beliefs and are influenced by our past experiences, our present circumstances, and our future aspirations. Getting clear on your values as a business owner is one of the most essential elements for creating a business that sets you free.

We are far more likely to fall out with someone about what they have or haven't done because of a values conflict than a personality conflict. Your business values must be the bedrock of who you are and how you want your business to function.

Just stating values however is not enough, you need to associate that value with the behaviours that you want to see and those you don't want to see. This is where you must think about the 'Why' behind the value, so everyone knows and understands how the value fits in with the business objectives.

One of my core values is fairness, but my idea of fairness may be very different to yours, so I need to expand on what fairness looks like in behavioural terms. I believe fairness is about treating everyone with the same respect and not allowing personal biases to influence my decisions.

The more clearly you can define your values, the easier it will be to describe the behaviours you want to see. Establishing behaviours that you don't want to see and then describing them in a positive way is most effective; instead of "don't be late", it's better to use "be punctual".

You need to decide on how many core values you are going to adopt; no more than six I suggest, as the more there are, the less likely they are going to stick in everyone's mind. You can involve your team with setting your values, but as the business owner, it's important that you have the final say.

Summary
What problem are you solving?
The Crossroads Model
The Five elements Model
The Role of a Coach
Create a Motivated Vision
Make it Visual
Track your progress
Who not How
Values, not Rules
For extra resources visit **www.motivatedthebook.com**

Action

CHAPTER 5:

Action – Bring Your Vision to Life

Introduction

Once you have decided on your direction, it's now time to put your plan into action; this chapter is about how to start on the right foot. This is where we need to be visible, noticing what's going on, nip any problems in the bud and reinforce what we want to see.

This can often be the most challenging stage as you and your team are adapting to the new direction or way of doing things. It's easy to get frustrated and end up going back to the old way as an easy option; this needs to be avoided.

Remembering the importance of High Challenge and High Support, you're not there to solve all the problems. You will no doubt be tested by some of the team who have not quite bought in and would prefer to return to the status quo.

Setting Goals

Now you are clear about your vision, you need to set some targets/goals around the key objectives you want to achieve by a future date. We tend to be overly optimistic about what we can achieve in a year but underestimate what we can achieve in a decade.

Think of a date in the future, 3/5/10 years' time, what will your business look like then? Do you aspire to be like another business in your sector, what would it take to be like them? What role will you have when everything is working like clockwork?

You may have aspirations to sell your business and move on to something completely different or even retire. There are many reasons to grow a business, what's your reason?

At what stage is your business? In his book "The E-Myth Revisited: Why most small businesses don't work and what to do about it", Michael E Gerber defines three stages, infant, adolescent and mature.

The infant business is one that is run by the owner and doesn't have any plans to grow, the drawbacks at this stage are that everything revolves around the owner. To move to the next stage of adolescence, the owner needs to learn to manage and be more strategic. The final stage is maturity, when you learn to step back and let others do the jobs you used to do.

Transitioning from one stage to the other is challenging as you need to learn new skills, adapt your mindset, and give up things you enjoy doing. If you are to remain motivated, you will need to recognise what you are good at and want to do and delegate the rest.

Break down the elements in your business that you need to develop to enable you to transition to the next stage, what do you want to achieve along the way? Here are a few things to think about.

Let's start with the numbers. What will your turnover need to be? What will your net profit be? How much will you be taking home? If you struggle with the financials, it may be time to find yourself a part-time finance director to guide you.

How many staff will you have? How many sites will you have? How many customers will you have? What awards do you want to win? How will you celebrate key milestones? How will your product/service develop?

Now, break down each of those goals into yearly segments. To achieve x turnover in five years, we will need to achieve this in year one, this in year two etc. It's a good idea to make this visual by using a flowchart or a group of decreasing circles.

Share your plans with everyone key to your business, including your suppliers and customers. By doing this, you get them on board early, and they may have some ideas that will enhance your plan.

Setting Expectations

Do you remember when the Spice Girls sang, "I'll tell you what I want, what I really, really, really want"? Being explicit with your language and making it clear what, how and why we do things in the way we do is an important skill to master.

In their book 'Liberating Leadership', Dr Derek Biddle & Ali Stewart outline the importance of being explicit and avoiding ambiguity. They identified that highly effective leader developers used the skill of defining and communicating in unambiguous behavioural terms exactly what is required.

This is a rarely taught skill and is seldom mentioned in management books; learning how to communicate what you want and don't want will set you apart. We tend to assume people know certain things, so we don't mention them, especially if someone is experienced.

Let's look at a situation with two different approaches, which one is clear and explicit?

"Your performance in the meeting with the client yesterday left a lot to be desired, I hope it was a one-off and next time you take a more active role."

"I'd like to reflect on how the meeting went yesterday, I didn't think you played an active role. Can I suggest you remove unnecessary distractions next time by leaving your phone in the car, that way you will be able to contribute like I know you can with your valuable knowledge of our systems."

Which one is likely to get a change in behaviour? By thinking about what we want to happen and then communicating in behavioural terms we are more likely to get the change in behaviour we want.

If something is not happening as you want it done, first ask "was I explicit enough?", and then define in behavioural terms what needs to change. It's worth mentioning that the only things we can expect to change in someone else are their behaviours or attitudes.

We've already looked at the importance of values to us and our personalities, the way we do things, is equally important and not for you to change. By keeping any performance issue at the behaviours and attitudes level, you avoid making it personal.

This is another reason why setting clear values that you follow can help you in situations where things aren't going so well. Having a conversation about acting against the core values of the business helps to avoid unnecessary references to personality traits that would likely cause offence.

The Onion Model is a useful analogy to remember, cutting too deep into an onion can feel uncomfortable and is best avoided.

Onion model

Like an onion is made up of many layers, people too have many layers made up of their personality, values, attitudes, and behaviours. Personality and Values are not what we want to seek to change; this would be cutting too deep.

By showing positive regard, we are respecting the individual and having a positive belief in them as a person. If we are unhappy about performance, we must only ever want to address behaviours and attitudes that are proving unhelpful.

Personality is someone's inner being, criticising is likely to receive a negative response.

Values are a person's deep-seated beliefs, as we explored in the last chapter, and are not readily changed.

Attitudes are underlying beliefs that underpin behaviours, we can change our attitude to something if we change our point of view.

Behaviours are what people do, are visible to all and can vary depending on the situation.

Remember when you are making comments about what's happening, it's about what they do, not who they are.

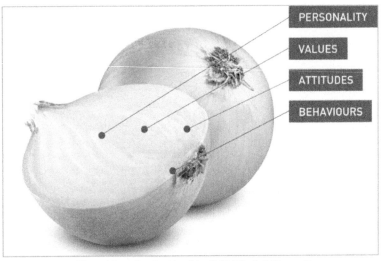

"From Liberating Leadership, D Biddle & A Stewart"

Who's accountable?

Your skills of explicitness will serve you well when you are deciding on who is accountable for what and describing what that accountability means to the business. We've looked at the importance of having someone to keep us accountable in chapter one; everyone involved in your business needs to know what they are accountable for.

By sticking to the concept of 'Who not How', you will accumulate a team around you that has the right skills to do the job. What we need to instil in the team is where they fit in and what important function they fulfil.

Create an accountability chart so that everyone can see where they fit in; this will help to establish an understanding of who is relying on who and like the Business Canvas, any new recruits will be able to see who does what.

Your role, unless you have delegated the task to someone else, is to keep everyone accountable and manage how the team are interacting with each other. If you are feeling at this point, 'Do I have to manage people?', then your motivation to control people and resources is probably quite low, which you need to reflect on.

The other key positions in the business are likely to be Sales/Marketing, Operations and Finance; each role needs to be clearly defined so responsibilities are clear. If you have a large enough team, you would make everyone accountable to one of these positions.

Each position should then take responsibility for the appropriate goals you have set, and each person responsible to that position will have their own targets to contribute to achieving the goals.

You've got to see it to believe it

At this point in the process, it's important to be visible and notice what's going on so you witness things as they develop and aren't relying on other people to tell you.

Relying on just what you have said and expecting it all to fall into place is overly optimistic and potentially naïve.

There are two reasons for this. Firstly, you need to assertively bring people back on track a soon as possible before bad habits form. If something has been misinterpreted, then you need to reassess how you have communicated your vision. Assertiveness is not being aggressive or passive, it comes from a place of respect for the individual and accepting that they are doing their best.

It's easy to get frustrated when things are not going as you had hoped; having strategies that help us in these situations is important. One of those strategies is the 'OK Corral', a model that takes into account how you view yourself and the other person. This comes from 'Transactional Analysis' by Eric Berne

I'm OK: your self-esteem is good and you feel in control
I'm not OK; you're not comfortable dealing with this issue, you're not coping
You're OK; you have a right to your opinions, you are a good person
You're not OK; you don't listen, you are wrong, you won't win this one

We need to operate from a position of 'I'm OK, You're OK' to be productive and avoid the negative connotations that could result. You have control of how you think about yourself and others; this is about being conscious of how you are feeling and how you are reacting.

Secondly, is to catch people doing things right so you can reinforce that good behaviour and confirm that it's the right thing. If we fail to notice and comment, then we have missed an opportunity to give positive feedback; we don't want to be the person who only notices when things are wrong.

There are several references to feedback in this book, the reason being it's the only way we know how we are doing. By making giving and receiving feedback an essential part of your culture, you're sending the message that we are all learning.

You will need resilience to overcome the frustrations, knowing what gives you energy, having a clear vision and playing to your strengths with help you maintain momentum. You will be challenged by some people, sometimes just by the way they do things. Remember, it's what they do that allows you to do what you do.

There are only two reasons why someone doesn't perform a task, either it's a 'won't', or a 'can't do'. 'Won't do' is an attitude problem as long as what they are being asked to do is reasonable. 'Can't do' is a skills issue, and the question to ask is, do I train them or give the task to someone else that does have the skills?

Stretch out, don't burn out

We all need a bit of stress in our lives to operate at our best; the problem comes when the stress becomes too much and we risk burnout or we risk rust out where we have a lack of stimulation and boredom sets in.

Stress is a stimulus that makes us take action when challenges arise, or a perceived threat is detected. We are all different, so finding the right level of stress for you and what you find stressful is what matters.

If we are to grow and fulfil our full potential, we must be prepared to leave our comfort zone and stretch ourselves. The first step is deciding on what you are going to give a go that slightly terrifies you.

A situation I mentioned in chapter one that many avoid as they perceive it as something as scary as death, is public speaking. I must admit that after my first experience, described in chapter one, it wasn't something I wanted to do again in a hurry.

What changed was I decided one day that it had the potential to open doors for me and allow me to make more of a difference. Sometimes we just need to associate something we are not motivated by with something that does.

I went on public speaking courses before I did my first speaking slot at a local networking event. Even though I had spent a fair amount of time learning how to do it, it would never be the same as the real thing. My knees were practically knocking together, and as soon I got up, I wanted it to be over.

Like learning to ride a bike, you've got to keep practising, and if you fall off, dust yourself down and give it another go. The worst thing that can happen is someone judges you, don't let one person's comments hold you back.

I've now spoken at many events, and I look forward to the next time because I've built up the confidence of knowing how it feels and how to manage it. Instead of feeling the fear, I make it a feeling of excitement and connecting to the opportunities it may bring.

We will look at some other factors that can contribute to stress and how to manage them in the next chapter.

You won't always have the answer

One mistake I made was thinking I should have the answer to all the problems and take responsibility for solving them myself. It was my overly supportive style kicking in and not realising I should be sharing the responsibilities and challenging my team to come up with solutions.

The first step to take is to admit you don't have an answer...yet. Showing some vulnerability with your team and having the courage to acknowledge that you're not perfect will connect you. I've heard it said that the reason Batman is seemingly more popular than Superman is likely to be that Batman has flaws.

Brene Brown is an American researcher who has written books on the importance of Vulnerability, and her Ted Talk on the subject has had over fifteen million views. Letting go of who you should be and embracing who you really are is the most authentic way to lead your business.

In her book 'The Gifts of Imperfection', Brene identifies 10 Guideposts for living imperfectly

Letting go of what people think
Letting go of perfectionism
Letting go of numbing and powerlessness
Letting go of scarcity and fear of the dark
Letting go of the need for certainty
Letting go of comparison
Letting go of exhaustion as a status symbol
Letting go of anxiety as a lifestyle
Letting go of self-doubt and "supposed to"
Letting go of being cool and "always in control"

These are all pressures we put on ourselves, not ones people are expecting of us; which ones can you let go? If you are going to create a business that sets you free, I'm sure these principles are worth adopting.

Find your Purpose

During the period after selling my retail business and setting up my coaching business, I sampled what it would be like to retire. I realised that having no responsibilities is just as bad as having too many; we all need a purpose to get out of bed in the morning.

This point was brought home to me a while ago when I popped in to wish one of my former employees' happy birthday. She had not long lost her husband after a long illness; she had been his carer for many years.

She spoke about how she just wanted him back and how she was struggling to come to terms with losing him. I realised that she was feeling like I did after handing the keys to the business over; she had lost her purpose.

When we have a purpose, we feel we are making a contribution and giving something back. Your business is an opportunity to connect to a cause that is much bigger than you; picking one of the UN 17 sustainable development goals is one way you can do that **www.sdgs.un.org/goals**

Another way could be to contribute to local good causes. Our retail business had its own 'making a difference locally' fund, which anyone could apply to for funding for small projects. Getting involved with fundraising is good fun, shows you want to make a difference and also raises your profile to your audience.

Having a clear purpose will help attract the right people who want to work for a business that is in touch with the needs of the wider community. A motivated business is one that is connected to a purpose much bigger than itself.

<u>Summary</u>
Setting goals
Setting Expectations
The Onion Model
Who's accountable
You've got see it to believe it
Stretch out don't burn out
You won't always have the answer
Find your purpose
For extra resources visit **www.motivatedthebook.com**

Systemise

CHAPTER 6:

Systemise – Create the Systems and Processes to Run the Business

Introduction

If you are going to create a business that will set you free, you need to have systems that will run it and, like the dashboard of a car, a way to monitor how it's doing. By using the information gathered, you can streamline your operation and keep costs under control.

You may not think you are busy enough to think about systemising, but this could be the perfect time to start jotting down the processes you are using. This is where explicitness is going to help you by being clear about what, how and why each part of the system is needed.

The best decision I made in our retail business was to computerise the ordering system using our Electronic Point of Sale (EPOS) system. Many retailers in the early days of EPOS only used their system to control prices; I saw the potential to use it as a stock control system. Not only did we save many hours of time creating orders, the orders were more accurate and reduced our stockholding, which reduced costs.

Measure what Matters

I mentioned in Chapter one that I like to go to HIIT sessions to keep myself fit; one of the things that keeps me going back is I measure my activity using a heart monitor that measures my effort and is connected to the systems that run the class, I gain points and a measurement of how I'm doing.

There's a target to reach each week and each month, and if I'm consistent, I get recognised by being awarded a higher level of achievement. Knowing how I'm doing and what I need to do to achieve the recommended amount of exercise allows me to manage my time accordingly.

Deciding what matters in your business and then measuring it will be crucial to its success; in his book 'Measure what Matters', John Doerr tells the story of introducing OKRs, Objectives and Key Results, to Google in its early days.

Without OKRs, Google's visionary founders had lots of energy and ideas but no idea how to turn them into a business. This is a common problem for creative entrepreneurs who enjoy idea creation but don't particularly enjoy routine.

Doerr talks about the four superpowers of OKRs

Focus and Commit to Priorities – deciding on what's most important for the next 3, 6 or 12 months, the objective is what we want to achieve, and the key results are how we choose to get there

Align and Connect for Teamwork – everyone has a personal OKR that contributes to the business OKR; make them visible for all to see

Track for Accountability – check in regularly with how you are doing, score your percentage progress

Stretch for Amazing – Be bold, think big

Your key motivations will determine what part of this process you connect to. For instance, if stability and predictability are important (Defender) you'll probably like the thought of being able to measure and track what's going on. If you like to feel connected to others (Friend), you will like that OKRs are shared, which connects your purpose, and if you like to be competitive (Builder), you will like the results-driven focus.

On the other hand, if you like to work autonomously (Spirit), it may feel like you are being restricted. If this is the case, you need to connect to the long term freedom that introducing a system around setting clear objectives and key results will give you.

Back in my retail days, we were able to monitor many of the financials in our business, the key ones being turnover and profit margin. There's a saying in retail that's relevant to all businesses, turnover is vanity and profit is sanity.

Knowing and understanding your numbers is essential; you need to keep a close eye on what's coming in and what's going out. I recommend getting a bookkeeper on board as soon as possible, so you and your accountant have access to up to date figures.

My father was obsessed with knowing what we had taken each day; if he didn't know, he would make sure he found out. This rubbed off on me, and it became a habit that I tracked sales against the previous week and the corresponding week of the previous year.

Don't make the mistake of thinking you are doing well just because you see money rolling into your bank account. You have to make sure those sales are profitable by firstly setting the right price based on a percentage profit margin and then taking into account the costs of supply.

Remember also that you have taxes to pay, and, in the case of value-added tax in the UK, they must be paid at the appropriate time. It's a good idea to set this money aside into another account that can't be easily accessed; after all this money does not belong to you and should not be spent.

Other things we can measure are the number of customers we have, are they increasing or decreasing, how many enquiries are we getting from our marketing each week? If we are dealing with physical products, either manufacturing or distributing, we can measure productivity levels and stock levels.

There's one other important factor in your business that you should consider measuring, how are your people feeling about their role? You could use a staff survey for this or an online diagnostic; Motivational Maps includes a fulfilment level for each of the motivators that is a really useful insight to what is important and how well those things are being met for everyone in the business.

Whatever is important to your business, make sure you have processes in place to measure it so you can make informed decisions.

Meetings with outcomes

Another benefit of OKRs is that they can be used to make every meeting productive and focused on outcomes. We've all had the experience of sitting through meetings that we didn't need to be at or have dragged on for far longer than they needed to.

Meetings should have a clear purpose for everyone who attends and an overall focus on solving problems. Don't try to solve every problem as it's raised, make a list and then prioritise, take action on what matters most at the time.

Learning to run effective meetings will save you lots of time in the long run; having a set format that works for you is important. I could give you a set structure that I would recommend, but that would only be what works for me.

Make the format the same each time, so everyone knows what to expect and how they are expected to contribute. Make sure they always finish on time, and you have agreed what needs to happen before your next meeting.

The next meeting should always start with everyone checking in with how they've done since the last one. Keep checking in with your team to offer support and encouragement, being mindful not to micromanage.

If you don't spend enough time planning your meetings and what outcomes you want from them, you will find they can easily become unproductive. Managing how meetings are managed and making sure you don't get bogged down in the detail is essential.

My father was not a fan of meetings due to the negative experience he had in a corporate environment, consequently we didn't have many, and If we did they were crisis meetings. Bringing people together can be logistically challenging and have a short term effect on productivity, but don't let that put you off.

The technologies to run effective online meetings have come on in leaps and bounds during the pandemic lockdowns, making it much easier to run engaging meetings with people in different locations. The thing to remember is to keep them short, snappy and engaging, so everyone looks forward to them instead of wishing they could avoid them.

Controlling your workload

Before looking at how we can reduce the number of tasks we need to do, I want you to reflect on how supportive and how challenging you are. If you are more supportive than challenging, a question I would ask is, "are you doing things for your team that you shouldn't be doing? Are they overly dependent on you?"

It's easy to create work for ourselves that we shouldn't be doing just because it makes life easier for your team. This is OK on the odd occasion when something needs to be done urgently, but if it's become a regular occurrence, you need to think about whether your expectations are high enough.

I say this from experience, as I've mentioned, I feel I was far too supportive and not challenging enough, which meant I took on tasks that someone else should have been doing.

Typically, they were tasks that I could do easily and enjoyed but were not what I should have been spending my time on.

At the same time, we don't want to encourage everyone to make their own decisions and carry them out without a thought for the implications to others and the business as a whole. We don't want dependence or independence, we want interdependence where everyone is self-reliant but also work with others collaboratively.

There are also some traps we need to avoid, such as blaming, being the hero, and I'm trying my best. These indicate you are operating from a position of lacking resources that are often available if you look and ask.

One of the biggest time wasters is being disorganised and not anticipating what will be needed and when. Prioritising your time and being realistic with what you can do in the time frame available is an important skill to master. Other problems arise from being impulsive and allowing interruptions that eat up your time and make you unproductive.

If you are not a naturally organised person, there is plenty of help out there; a Virtual Assistant is naturally good at organising and often motivated by creating structure and systems. The time you create can be better spent developing and motivating your team and taking time to think strategically about where the business is going.

The Eisenhower Matrix

US President Dwight D. Eisenhower supposedly once said. *"The most urgent decisions are rarely the most important ones"* Eisenhower was considered a master of time management, he seemed to have the ability to do everything as and when it needed to be done.

When you have many tasks that need to be done, and you don't know where to start, break down each task into one of four options. In the diagram, you will see two axis, one labelled 'Important', and the other 'Urgent', and each axis has a positive and negative or, in other words, urgent/not urgent, important/not important.

You can segment each of your tasks into the four quadrants, not important and not urgent, important and not urgent, urgent and not important and urgent and important. You now know whether to do it immediately, decide when you will do it, do it later or delegate to somebody else.

This is also a good way to decide on which OKRs need to be prioritised and which ones can wait.

	Urgent	Not Urgent
Important	**Do** Tasks with clear deadlines and significant consequences in not completed in a timely fashion.	**Schedule** Tasks with no set deadline but that bring you closer to your long-term goals.
Not Important	**Delegate** Tasks that need to get done but don't need your expertise in order to be completed.	**Delete** Tasks that distract you from your preferred course, and don't add any measurable value.

"Eisenhower Matrix by Stephen Covey"

Automate

If your business is going to set you free, you need to think about how you can automate the processes in your business. This may sound obvious, but, in my experience, it can easily be put off for too long.

I shared in the chapter introduction how taking that extra step that most people don't take can make a big difference. Driven by my motivation of creativity and making a difference, I introduced an end to end process that saved hours of work each week.

When considering what to automate first, you can use a similar process to the Eisenhower Matrix using Time and Cost as the axis. The task with the most time-saving potential and costing the least to implement being the one to start with.

A good way to work out whether something is worth implementing would be how fast you will get a return on your investment. Make sure you account for your own time at an appropriate hourly rate based on the salary of replacing you.

Let's take software, which is a considered purchase that will automate a process in your business. The cost would include the purchase price of the software, any specialist help to get the system set up correctly, training of staff, possible reduction in productivity short term and on-going support costs.

Work out the potential cost savings by using the hourly rates for everyone that will benefit in the first year and then divide the total cost to implement by the first year's savings. The number you get is the amount of years it will take to pay for the investment.

One thing I highly recommend you use is a calendar booking system, this has been the biggest time saver for my coaching business. Some people get a bit snooty about it and say it is impersonal, which I would agree with if you just send a link without a short explainer.

I have links set up for all my different client services, 1-2-1 follow up calls, and my live get savvy show guest slots; they all are set up for different durations and times of availability and save, what I call, the messaging tennis.

I also use a cloud accounting system connected to my bank account to retrieve all transactions that then just need to be given a transaction code that identifies what it was for and the relevant invoice attached.

This was something we had nailed in our retail business too, and included our payroll system, which was also automated using a fingerprint signing in system. This allowed us to check attendance with the staff rota, which reduced errors and saved time checking timesheets.

The payroll system was connected to our accountancy system which connected to our bank account to make the payments. From paying cash weekly to paying by bank transfer monthly, we saved two days' work every month, the payback was less than six months, I seem to remember.

It's important to get everyone on board before you start to introduce a new system; I made the mistake of pushing ahead with computerising our accounts without getting the support of our office manager. All my enthusiasm wasn't going to persuade someone who just thought I was trying to make him redundant.

Marketing is a key function of your business that can be automated; marketing needs to be consistent to be effective, so automating it makes good sense. Creating a content calendar that everyone can contribute to is a good way of connecting everyone to your marketing message.

By focusing on the right things to automate, you will save yourself lots of time and create what is called a turnkey operation. This is the principle that business franchises work on, create a system that works and then sell the system to others to use.

Probably the most well-known business franchise is McDonald's, everything in that business has a process to follow. Not only does it save time, it also creates consistency so a customer knows what they will get whichever branch they walk into.

Productising your offer

I don't know whether you've noticed but renting is becoming the norm when it comes to many things in our lives. We used to buy a CD with a copy of the software we needed, pop it in the computer and install it. Nowadays, we download the software for free and then decide on what level of subscription we need.

With this model, you don't get to own the software, you rent it until you decide to stop paying your monthly subscription. Commonly referred to as the Netflix model, access is granted to all the content you want at a low monthly cost instead of selling each film or program separately.

You can now subscribe to products like unlimited coffee, flower bouquets, meal plans, razor blades and services like how to play a musical instrument, how to cook and how to cut hair.

This business model is becoming more popular due to the regular income it generates for the business and the flexibility it offers by spreading the cost for the customer. Check your next card statement and see how many subscriptions you have going out each month.

How could you create a membership subscription that your customers could subscribe to instead of, or as an additional service?

Work smart 80:20

All things are not equal when it comes to running a business, if everything we did gave a corresponding amount of benefit, we could just work harder and the result would match our effort. In a similar way to how the Eisenhower Principle works, we need to decide what activities contribute the most to our effectiveness.

The Italian-born economist Vilfredo Pareto when studying the distribution of wealth, discovered that eighty per cent of the wealth was held by twenty per cent of the people. It's since been noticed that this principle can be used in many parts of our lives and business because around eighty per cent of our results come from twenty per cent of our activities.

If we want to create a business that sets us free, we need to focus on the twenty per cent that will get eighty per cent of the results. Instead of just working harder, we need to work smarter on what will make the biggest difference each day.

In their book 'Mapping Motivation for Leadership', James Sale and Jane Thomas suggest there are five elements that we need to focus on, Thinking, Doing, Team Building, Motivating and Self Development. I have covered the importance of self-development in part one of this book, so let's look at the other four elements.

Let's break down each of these elements starting with Thinking. In Chapter Four, Evaluate, we looked at the importance of a motivated vision and values, which are thinking activities. Other thinking activities would be planning, problem-solving and innovating; where do you do your best thinking?

We tend to do our best thinking when we are in a relaxed state, I have found that the golf course is a good place for me. Find the place where you do your best thinking and make time for it.

Doing is not for doing's sake but purposeful doing that moves you towards your vision. Managing and prioritising your time and running productive meetings with clear outcomes are doing activities we have looked at in this book.

Another key doing activity is recruiting the right people, retaining them and sometimes removing them. If you are going to create a business that sets you free, the people you employ will have a major impact on allowing or preventing that from happening.

The final two elements of Team Building and Motivating will be covered in part three of this book, where we look at how to create a Motivated Team.

Your habits become your character

We looked at the importance of developing our character in chapter two; let's take a closer look at the character strengths that will make the biggest impact. Some of these will be natural strengths, and some may be ones you need to spend time developing.

Systemising is not just about how we do things, it's also about how we are being; by being, I mean how we are showing up.

If we can develop the character traits that allow us to be who we want to be, we are more likely to create a way of being that makes all the things we need to do just part of who we are.

It's also important to encourage others to show up as the best version of themselves so they can develop the character strengths they naturally have and use. Catching people doing things right is important; just as important is catching people being the person they want to be.

One of the most satisfying parts of running our retail business was employing 15-16-year-olds in most cases in their first job, and then seeing them grow and become full-time employees or leave and go to university. With that in mind, I'm going to share what I see as the key character strengths I needed to allow that to happen.

The first character strength is forgiveness, when I completed a Character strengths assessment, it was number one which surprised me; but on reflection, it's something I took for granted. Allowing people to make mistakes and forgiving them is a powerful way to transfer a feeling of trust.

Giving people a second chance and not being vengeful will allow the person to realise that the important thing about mistakes is preventing them from happening again. We need to guard against overly using our character strengths; in the case of forgiveness, it would be to become a doormat and allow everything to pass without questioning and challenging.

Another of my top strengths turned out to be perspective which is my ability to step back and see the bigger picture. It's easy to react to what's happening today, we need to control that reaction so it doesn't undermine our future plans. It's about stopping and thinking, how important will this be in a month or year from now.

If we focus on the elements we have control over and accept that things outside of our control may disrupt our plans, however frustrating that may be, we give ourselves the best chance of success. One thing we always have control over is how we react to events which is another important character strength, self-regulation.

The next character strength that has served me well is optimism or hope, as it is described by my VIA character strengths assessment. It's my second strongest trait; although I would never have described myself as optimistic, when I think back, I was good at staying positive and not letting setbacks get me down.

Optimism is one of seven characteristics that have been identified as ones that lead to better academic achievement, success, and happiness. The other six are gratitude, social intelligence, curiosity, self-control, enthusiasm, and perseverance.

What are your natural character strengths? Which ones do you need to work on to help you create a business that sets you free? You can take the VIA Character survey here **www.viacharacter.org**

Summary
Measure what matters
Meetings with outcomes
Controlling Your workload
The Eisenhower Matrix
Automate
Productising your offer
Work smart 80:20
Your habits become your character

For extra resources visit **www.motivatedthebook.com**

PART THREE: MOTIVATED TEAM

Your Team will be the key to creating a business that sets you free so we need to pay particular attention to how we do that. A motivated team will be fully bought into your vision and know where they fit in and the role they play.

You know how important it is that your role motivates you and keeps your energy high, each and every member of your team needs the same. Being consciously aware of the key motivator of your team will allow you to reward them in the way they prefer.

Teams are more than a group of people brought together; we want everyone to achieve more because they are part of the team, 'Together Each Achieves More'. We know that the best teams on paper based on abilities alone quite often fail to reach their potential.

In this part of the book, we will look at the U. R. E. elements of the MEASURE process.

Unify

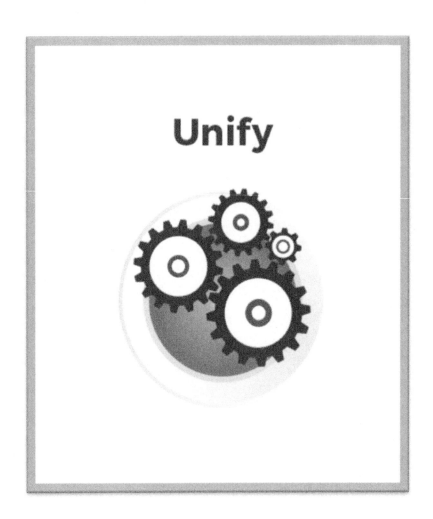

CHAPTER 7:

Unify – Develop A Team to Take Your Vision Forward

Introduction

Your role is to focus on what your team needs from you to perform at their best, we have covered the elements of thinking and doing in part two; in this part, we will look at motivating and building your team.

A key area you need to focus on is the energy within your team, the higher the energy level, the greater the chance of success. Our energy levels are dependent on doing the things that give us that energy and avoiding where possible the tasks that sap our energy.

To perform at our best, we need to be highly skilled, highly motivated and know how we contribute to the success of the business. By learning to how to positively influence everyone in your business using effective listening, encouraging co-operation and developing everyone's abilities you will free up your time for your most important tasks.

Create your motivated tribe

When you have a clear idea about your own motivations, and you've created a motivated business idea, the final step is to inspire a tribe to follow you because you want to do things differently.

Seth Godin, the author of many marketing books, also wrote 'Tribes, we need you to lead us'; notice it's not manage us.

Having the mindset of building a tribe instead of a workforce will help you when it comes to attracting the right people.

A tribe is a group of people connected to one another, connected to a leader, and connected to an idea. You can't have a tribe without a leader, and you can't be a leader without a tribe.

A tribe is connected by a belief that something is worth doing and can be achieved by working with others. People want to belong to a tribe that they believe in and also buy from businesses that they believe in.

Leading a tribe is not about taking responsibility, it's about creating possibility and showing a way to change something. It will depend on a clear message that is well communicated so everyone is engaged in the vision.

Your tribe is more than your team, it includes your customers who see why you do what you do. It also includes your suppliers who know where they fit in and how they play their part in bringing your vision to life.

Be the guide not the Boss

Being the boss is part of being a business owner but can feel uncomfortable if you're not motivated by being in charge. By seeing yourself as more a guide than a boss, you can release some of the pressure that comes with the role.

A guide is someone who shows the way and influences development and behaviours. We have looked at the importance of only ever wanting to change attitudes and behaviours, and this fits the guide's role perfectly.

I can remember times running my retail business when I was the guide, it felt comfortable and less of a burden than being the boss. My behavioural style is people-focused so this fits with my natural style. If you have a more task-focused behavioural style, Red and Blue, you may find this less intuitive.

When we are on a city break, we can buy a map of the city and find our own way around. When we join a guided tour, we have the added benefit of someone who will show us the best parts and is there to answer questions. They won't have all the answers, but they will be able to shortcut to where to find the answer.

I first came across the guide concept in Donald Miller's 'Building a Story Brand' book where he talks about being the guide, not the hero. A guide has a plan to follow and will challenge you to take action; you can create heroes by being the guide to your tribe.

If leadership is about influencing others to want to follow us, Marketing is about influencing others to buy into our product or service. There are many similarities that Leadership and Marketing have in common; I believe the most important is realising that motivation plays a vital role in whether we are successful.

There's nothing wrong with being a boss, someone has to be 'in charge'; being in charge comes with a responsibility to those you lead and manage. What we need to guard against is being in charge for just the power or recognition it gives us.

I ended up 'in Charge' not because I had aspirations to manage but because I was the one who had ideas that pushed the business forward. I guess I showed leadership qualities of not waiting for someone to tell me what to do, I just got on and did what I thought was the right thing.

A trap we can fall into is having a preconceived idea about what being the boss is about and how we should behave. My only experience of working for someone was when my father was still involved with our retail business. His style was very different to mine, more task-focused whereas I'm more people-focused.

As you will discover in this part of the book, you can lead your own way, you just need to follow the process.

Adapt your style to the situation

The process I mention is the four-step process from 'Liberating Leadership' by Dr Derek Biddle and Ali Stewart, which are Visioning, Mobilising, Developing and Enabling. We have covered Visioning and Mobilising in the previous two chapters, Developing and Enabling are the next two steps.

Developing is the part of the process where you can start to step back a little, your team is getting into a groove, and things are happening without you always being there. You are getting to know your team's strengths and weaknesses and know what they need from you. Enabling is the final stage, you are delegating tasks and authority but still retaining responsibility for how things are going.

We looked at our behavioural styles using the four colour energies in chapter 3 when we held up the mirror. Those colour energies also have an influence on how we lead and at which point in the process we operate to our strengths. If we are to be effective, we need to learn to flex our style to suit the situation.

At the Visioning stage, we need to be quite direct and instructive about what we want to happen, how we are going to do it and why; this is where you could be at your best if you lead with red energy.

At the Mobilising stage, we need to notice what is going on and bring people back on track if they have strayed into bad habits—this is a more coaching style of talking things through and asking questions to solve problems. If you lead with Yellow energy, you may find this part of the process is your strength.

At the Developing stage your expertise is not needed so much, so you have more of a supporting or mentoring role to play. This could be where you could be strong if you lead with Green energy.

And finally, the Enabling stage where your team is fully able to function without your day to day involvement, this could be your strength if you lead with blue energy. I say could be because we can learn to act outside our natural style by training or using our own intuition from experiences and challenges we've overcome.

Something important to remember is that people join businesses at different times and at different points in the process. Depending on where that person is in the process, you need to adapt to their situation, not yours. We don't want to treat someone that has been in the business for two months the same as someone who has been there two years.

We will all have strong points in the process; mine are the Mobilising and Developing stages where coaching and mentoring is needed most. What you need to work on is using the right style and colour energy at the right time, which takes practice, and you won't get it right every time.

If you have a new starter with previous experience, it's tempting to skim over the first three steps and go straight to delegating. What's likely to happen is that they settle into bad habits that are not in line with your vision or values, make sure you always follow the process.

Embrace Your differences

We have covered in the first part of this book how to stay motivated, and in the second part how to create a motivated business idea. When building a motivated team, we need to look at things so we can embrace our differences and make them strengths not reasons for conflict.

You may have thought a motivated team is all about creating harmony and everyone going along with your point of view. A team is not a group of people who are like you, do things like you and are motivated by the same things as you. Creating a team means you have to have people with the right skills but also motivated to be in that role which, if it's not your ideal role, will need different skills and motivations.

Our family retail business was split across two sites, I ran one, and my brother ran the other. This came about when we purchased the second site and it was decided we would each have a store to manage. My brother had been working in our first store since leaving school and was ready for a new challenge and I was ready to step up and take more responsibility.

My brother and I are very different, his behavioural style is opposite to mine, and he is motivated by different things than me. Because of these differences we had our fair share of fallings out, which was always blamed on our personalities, but in hindsight, I think it was much more to do with our motivations that were in conflict.

Since starting my coaching business, I have spent a lot of time learning about behavioural styles and motivations. An important difference between the two is that behavioural styles don't tend to change much unless we are actively looking to change them, whereas motivations do change because they are affected by our self-perception and our future aspirations.

Our motivations are our motive to take action, the stronger the motive, the more we are likely to take action and vice versa. Each decision you make in your business is affected by your motivations and is why you gain energy from some things you do and feel the energy drain when doing others.

Motivations give us a purpose in what we do and a reason why what we do matters to us, to the overall goals of the team and the business. By harnessing the energy that everyone in the team gets from doing what gives them energy, you will create a team that embraces their differences.

In the latter days of running our retail business, we started to introduce responsibilities that were not just site-specific; if we had been more aware of our differing motivations at that time, I believe we could have been even more successful.

Manage your ego

Your ego is your sense of self-esteem or your self-importance, it's how we see ourselves and the image that we think we should portray to others. If we are going to be motivated in our role, we need to shake off any preconceived ideas that we need to be a particular way.

In his book 'The ego is the enemy', Ryan Holiday describes ego as *"an unhealthy belief in our own importance"* and can turn a concern about our self-image into an obsession that prevents us reaching long term goals.

Writing a book is a test of ego because it exposes us to other people's opinions of our work, deciding not to write a book is protecting our ego. On the other side of the ego balance, we can get overly confident because we have achieved success and start making rash decisions.

Managing our ego is like balancing a seesaw, if we lean too much one way or the other, it can tip over. Allowing ourselves to make mistakes and not letting them prove that we are either great or useless is key.

Ego may show up when you start to feel your team doesn't really need you anymore, and because you feel left out, you could unintentionally sabotage what you're trying to achieve. You can also fall into a similar trap if you have been away from the business for a while and when you return, start looking for what's wrong rather than what's right.

If you have been reasonably successful in the past, your ego can stand in the way of allowing new innovations because they haven't been proven. My father was adamant that we didn't need to introduce electronic point of sale because we had been successful without it.

None of us like to admit that we are wrong, so we protect ourselves from having to do so, which sometimes shows up when we are trying to retain the status quo. Our ego is a feeling, we can learn to manage that feeling so it doesn't become a barrier to our success.

Sharing is caring

The more we know about people, the more we are likely to trust them, so a culture of sharing things about ourselves with our team will develop that trust. This isn't about telling everyone your darkest secrets, it's about showing your human side.

If you have a strong relationship motivation, this will be something you're probably doing naturally because of your drive for connection and belonging. If you're motivated more by the growth motivators, it may be something you need to be more conscious about.

Simple things like sharing what you did at the weekend is a good way of finding out a bit more about your team as most will share their own weekend experiences. Sharing when you are having a tough time is also important so they understand that if you're not your usual self-it's nothing to do with what they have or haven't done.

Sharing our behavioural styles and motivations with the team is a great way to increase understanding and connect to what each person brings to the team. The tools I use for identifying behavioural styles and motivations have a team function where you can show the individual preferences and how they fit with the team.

The colour behavioural style model is ideal for sharing a language around how we prefer to show up and perform tasks. By sharing this with others, we encourage everyone to appreciate one another for their strengths and accept their weaknesses.

When we know our own and the style of the other person, we can adapt so we increase our level of rapport and can communicate better. When we don't understand someone's way of doing things, we can easily assume they are just being difficult. When we know that it's just their way of doing things, we can accept neither of us is right or wrong.

I'm often copied into email exchanges that my clients are sending to their team, and it's fascinating how different the replies can be. If you have received a long email with lots of detail, the thing not to do is answer with one line, unless that is what has been asked for.

Someone with a high blue tendency is likely to be the one that has to share every detail, and a high red is likely to be the one that replies with a one-liner. You can see how this is not ideal when it comes to creating rapport because each is not taking the other person's preference into account.

We don't need to change to the other person's style but adapt so we are not communicating in completely different ways. It's kind of like when we go on holiday, if we make an effort to use some of the language native to the country, we are more likely to gain respect.

Behavioural styles team reports put each of the team's members into the colour segment that matches their strongest colour preference. This can then be shared with the team so they understand who is like them and who uses a different style. Those in the opposite quadrant are the people we will most likely have more challenges with as the way they do things could grate on us.

Sharing our motivations is another way we can better understand each other as this also indicates the type of things we see as rewards. If we can reward everyone so that their motivators are being fulfilled, it's a win for you and a win for them.

Motivational Maps can be used to create a motivational profile of the team by adding up the individual scores for each of the motivators into an overall score for the team. The motivators are then displayed from strongest to weakest in the form of a bar chart for you and the team to see.

You, as the business owner, can then use the report as a how-to guide when it comes to motivating your team. Rather than guessing and rewarding everyone the way you think they want, you can devise a strategy that suits the team and focuses on keeping them motivated.

It's also important to consider how each member of the team gets their motivators fulfilled from their role. This is where individual contributions to the team are important to connect with how they contribute to a worthwhile outcome.

One of my coaching clients was becoming disillusioned with her role as a conveyancing solicitor, and her motivational map indicated why. She was motivated to make a difference, so needed to know from feedback how she did that. Her manager wasn't forthcoming with feedback, so I suggested looking back at her client testimonials. She was able to identify that she was helping her clients to buy their next home that would transform their lives; that's what difference she was making.

Sharing the results of reports amongst the team will increase understanding, promotes interdependency and better communication.

Be visible, remote and approachable

If you are new to the concept of leading a team, you can make the mistake of remaining in the team rather than being the one showing the way. Having a buddy approach may feel good and may work for a while, but inevitably you will need to deal with performance issues and you may end up smoothing over rather than addressing any issues.

If you miss being part of the team, then you must find a new team to be part of, a mastermind group of like-minded business owners for example could bridge the gap.

You can alternatively take the position that I'm in charge now and start issuing instructions and procedures to follow.

In the first example we are showing positive regard but lacking the genuineness to give the necessary feedback. In the second example, we are lacking positive regard and likely to come across as dictatorial; we need to have a balance of Positive Regard and Genuineness.

I have to admit that I am more comfortable showing positive regard than genuineness, which often resulted in me flipping when frustrated to being genuine but lacking positive regard. What I've learnt since is using both, not one or the other, is where we need to operate; when we get the balance right, we create the space for trust and growth

Summary
Create a motivated tribe
Be the guide, not the boss
Adapt your style to the situation
Embrace your differences
Manage your ego
Sharing is caring
Be visible, remote, and approachable
For extra resources visit **www.motivatedthebook.com**

Review

CHAPTER 8:

Review – Checking and Reflecting

Introduction

An entrepreneurial mindset is great for getting things going, and without it, most businesses never get off the ground. As the business starts to find a rhythm, it's important to check that you are on track and making progress on what you set out to achieve.

Having an awareness of your motivations will help you with spending your time on things that give you energy, but what about the things that don't that are essential for your business success? This chapter is about what your business needs and your role is to identify are you likely to do it, or do you need to find someone else?

Checking is one of the elements of the Five Element model, as described in chapter four, that needs to be followed for the whole business and for individual projects within the business. Checking, you could say, is the least sexy of the five elements and the most likely to be neglected if it's the growth motivators are driving you.

Slowing down to speed up

If we always have our foot to the floor and never stop to check how we are doing, we are in danger of losing sight of what we set out to create, a business that sets us free. Being busy can make us feel that we are making progress, but without taking time to check and reflect, we could one day end up in a place we never wanted to be.

Taking time out to check how we are doing is essential and involves taking our foot off the accelerator, pulling over and checking where we are. There are bound to have been some blocked roads which we needed to navigate around, and new routes that have appeared that may be better than our original plan.

Your business should not be about being busy; being busy just for the sake of it will create a *busyness*, not a business that sets you free. Your time is your most precious commodity, it should be used wisely and is a crucial mindset to master if you want to avoid just creating a job for yourself.

Thinking time should be part of your routine, don't leave it to when you have time as that indicates it's not that important. If you only went on holiday when you had nothing else to do, then you'd never go on holiday, if it's in the diary you'll make it happen.

Our best thinking is done when we are relaxed, so I recommend you find a space where you are comfortable and won't be interrupted. I'm not going to tell you how you do this because what works for me may not work for you, it may take a bit of trial and error. I sometimes like to find a coffee shop that isn't too busy so I can watch the world go by; other times it can be somewhere quiet and off the beaten track.

The Change Curve

When we are working towards bringing our vision to life, there's an inevitable need for change, so we need to understand how change needs to be managed.

We also need to be aware of our attitude towards change and how it may differ from our team, because with change comes uncertainty and risk.

There is, of course, a difference between change that is imposed on us and is unplanned to the type of change we are looking for, which is in line with our vision. There may well be elements of our vision that our team may not be totally on board with and may have a bit of resistance to, which is why we need to be visible and observe what's really happening.

There are typically six stages of change that we go through, and the speed at which we move through them is dependent on the amount of encouragement, recognition and support we receive. It will also depend on whether we feel we have the right skills and how resilient we are with regards to coping.

Each of your team can be at different stages in the change cycle, which often starts with a sense of disbelief that it's happening and then moves to the next stage of denying it will have any effect. This is where your team needs you to be around for reassurance, so they don't get stuck and are able to move to the next stage.

When we are learning to do new things or accept the new situation, we are bound to feel uncomfortable and frustrated until we have had time to come to terms with what's happening. At this stage, performance is likely to be taking a dip due to the lack of certainty, and your role needs to be supportive by moving them through to acceptance.

Once the new reality has been accepted, you can then move to the testing stage where we start using a new way of working and accepting that making mistakes is part of the process. Finally, we get to a position of completion that is better than where we originally started, and the ability to ride the next wave of change is increased.

Reviewing where you are on the change curve gives a point of reference as to where we are and checking we are not leaving anyone behind. We all move through the change curve at different speeds. Your role as a business owner is to lead your team through the change, realising that not everyone will move at the same speed.

It's also important to recognise that you are also moving through this change curve and will need some support. Even though this is your business and vision, you will have times of doubt and may think about giving up, this is where having someone, like a business coach, to remind you of why you started in the first place is important.

"From Liberating Leadership, D Biddle & A Stewart"

Influencing Styles

If we are not getting the results we are looking for, it could well be that we need to think about the way we are influencing. Our behavioural style will have an influence on the way we tend to approach most situations, and, just as we need to adapt our leadership style to the situation, we need to adapt our influencing style.

Our ability to get things done will be dependent on how effective we are at influencing others to want to do what we need them to do. This plays out in many areas of our lives, whether we are negotiating with our partner as to where we are going on holiday, or who is buying the first round at the pub.

There are four main styles of Influencing, and a fifth which is moving away from a situation to avoid further discussion, either temporarily or permanently. The four influencing styles are Asserting, Persuading, Bridging and Attracting, and all have appropriate uses.

Asserting is where you communicate your own needs; Persuading is used when you need to convince others of the best course of action; Bridging is where you emphasise common ground and Attracting is painting a picture of possibilities and inspiring others.

Asserting and Persuading are what could be described as pushing styles, either pushing away or pushing in a particular direction. Bridging and Attracting are more pulling styles where you are taking the other person into account and making it what they want too.

Learning to use all the styles at the appropriate time will increase your ability to influence in all sorts of situations. Which style do you use most often, and which one takes you out of your comfort zone?

My own preferences are Bridging and Attracting, which are suited to my people-orientated behavioural style that prefers to avoid potential conflict. Asserting my own views is something I've learnt to do at the appropriate time but doesn't come naturally.

Establishing a Can't do or a Won't do

Influencing skills will help us to communicate our ideas more effectively, but what if that's not working? Identifying why someone isn't doing the things we want them to do boils down to either a 'can't do' or a 'won't do'.

To evaluate which one is at play, there are some questions we can ask ourselves always remembering to define things in terms of attitudes and behaviours only. In the 'Liberating Leadership' book, there's a flowchart called the 'Performance Navigator' which starts with five crucial questions.

Define the specific performance behaviour, including present undesirable and future desirable behaviours.

Do these reasons matter in terms of actual performance?

Do they know what is expected?
Describe what is required in explicit, behavioural terms, and monitor subsequent performance closely.

Is the person now performing well?

If the answer to number 5 is no, then the acid question is, "Could they do what is being asked if their life was dependent on it?" If the answer is NO, then it's a 'can't do' skills issue; if the answer is YES, then it's a 'won't do' attitude issue.

If you explore the lack of skills or lack of will and are not able to resolve the issue, it may just be the case that the person doesn't have the appropriate potential for the job and needs to be let go, harsh as it may seem.

How far have you come?

In chapter one, I stressed the importance of enjoying the journey and avoiding getting too focused on the outcome. It's important also to recognise how far you have come and what you have learnt along the way.

Each day is a school day, as they say, meaning we are always learning as we learn, we make progress, but this may not be visible. How we feel about our progress will be dependent on what's important to us, and that is where being in tune with our motivations is important.

Having a system of measuring achievements across all aspects of the business gives us a feeling of progress, so it's important to measure the things that mean the most to you. If you are only measuring the financial side of the business and money isn't something that's important to you, then you are not going to feel you are making the progress you want.

For instance, if you are motivated by being a specialist (the expert motivator) but the work you are getting is quite mundane, you're not going to feel you are making the progress you want. By checking in with this, you can make the adjustments needed to attract more of the type of work you really want.

A business balance sheet is a summary of all the assets of the business, what the business owns and what the business owes, which will often be created by an accountant. The balance sheet is a snapshot of the financial position of the business so you can see at a glance how, the business is progressing compared with last year.

Create a balance sheet of all the non-tangibles that are important to you, such as the difference you are making to your customers, the skills you are developing in your business and the community you are growing. By doing this, you are not focusing solely on the financials of the business but the business achievements as a whole.

Listening, the underrated skill

The power of listening, or giving someone a chance to speak and be heard, can never be underestimated; making ourselves available to listen can be one of the greatest gifts to another person. The Greek philosopher Epictetus said, "*We have two ears and one mouth so we can listen twice as much as we speak*", and Wilson Mizner, the American playwright, said, "*A good listener is not only popular everywhere, but after a while, he knows something*".

When running a business, we need to be listening to our customers to make sure we are living up to their expectations, and we also need to be listening to our employees so they feel they have a voice. According to the Macleod report, another key factor when creating an engaged workforce is employee voice.

Listening is something we need to learn how to do well because we all know how it feels when someone appears to be listening but is actually just passing the time of day. So, what makes a good listener, and how can we learn the skills that will help us make a positive impact?

Firstly, we need to be actively engaged in listening, which takes a level of conscious awareness of how we are listening. Listening can be a way just to gather the information we want to use, or it can be a way to connect with someone's thoughts and feelings. If we are not paying enough attention, we can miss non-verbal clues about what is actually being said and the meaning behind the words.

If we are really listening, rather than giving advice or answers, we will become curious and we will want to know more. To show you have been listening, paraphrasing what you have heard and then following up with another question can be effective. By doing this, you are putting yourself in the other person's shoes rather than just seeing your point of view.

The type of questions you ask is important to get right; closed questions that require a yes or no answer are not going to be useful in most situations. Questions should be open and probing to encourage more detail and dive a little deeper, for example, "Can you expand on that?"

By using good listening skills and probing questions, you can avoid jumping to conclusions when something hasn't gone to plan. Maintaining positive regard allows you to ask questions like "What was the problem?" which is recognising that you must have had a problem because it's unlike you; rather than just "Why are you late?" It's quite subtle but lands a lot better because it takes away the assumption that you messed up.

Another way to show you are listening and are also there to help, is to share your own mistakes with your team and how you changed your attitude or behaviour. Showing empathy that you have been there and made a similar mistake will help to build trust.

In Stephen Covey's book 'The 7 Habits of Highly Effective People' habit five is *"seek first to understand then to be understood"*. When you have the frame of mind of listening to others before making your point of view heard, you create empathy.

An opportunity we can create to listen to our team is by having a one to one appraisal meeting or, as we preferred to call them, job chats.

Motivated Job Chats

It's not important what you call them, what is important is that you have them, and you have a format to follow. One of the biggest learnings I took from the Investors in People process was that we needed to have regular structured staff check-ins. It seems obvious, but it's so easy to let them lapse when you are busy, if you do let them slip, you are sending out completely the wrong message.

Something to keep in mind when conducting any sort of performance appraisal is what William James, the American philosopher, remarked "*the deepest principle of human nature is the craving to be appreciated*", which gives feedback an even deeper meaning.

What needs to be avoided, and which is a common criticism of the appraisal process, is making it into just an opportunity to bring up past issues. We need to approach the process with an 'I'm Ok', 'You're Ok' mentality, which will promote a positive discussion and not one that leads to demoralisation.

When thinking about the elements we should be covering in our job chats, we first need to return to the Objectives and Key Results from chapter six and check progress. By checking progress towards the OKR, we are emphasising their importance and whether they contribute effectively towards the overall goals of the team and business.

This is also an opportunity for the team member to be involved in setting the OKRs and to revisit their job descriptions. I've lost count of the number of people that have told me that their job description does not reflect their role. This is a great opportunity to make sure everything is updated and relevant to the current situation.

A motivated job chat must also have a focus on the needs and wants of the team member, so we need to take into account what they are. The OKRs address the What and How we do what we do; the missing element is Why does it matter to them?

If we are clear about why things matter to us, we can then appreciate why something else matters to our team member. If something matters, it's a feeling that gives us a motive, the stronger the motive, the more likely we are to act.

Establishing the 'Why' is the element of the process that is often missing and why we don't get the buy-in from the team member. It can often feel like we are speaking different languages because we can only see it from the perspective of why it matters to us.

When I started the Reluctant Leader podcast, the idea was to invite guests to discuss leadership topics with experts in their field. What was just as important to me was getting to know why they did what they did; the passion behind many of the stories that were told brought home to me why our 'Why' is so important.

Motivational Maps is the ideal tool to identify and describe what is motivating each individual in the team and also measure how they feel their motivators are being fulfilled. We can then make sure that we set OKRs that are in line with the goals of the business and also motivate the person.

The three elements needed for a motivated job chat are to establish whether key motivations are being met, how are we are doing with regards to OKRs and to set future targets. By having a balanced approach to what the business needs and what the team member needs, you're much more likely to have a productive session that's a win-win for both parties.

Practice doesn't make perfect

Nothing can replace practice when leading a business, and as you probably know, there's never any shortage of people making their opinions known when something isn't to their liking. When reviewing how you are doing, it can feel like a rollercoaster with ups and downs, twists and turns and then ending up where you started.

Leading a business can be very rewarding one minute and then totally demoralising the next. When plans and expectations aren't being met, it's easy to feel that you're not cut out for the role; I had many occasions when I wondered why I bothered.

The reason why the first part of the book is all about Motivated You is that you need to be at your best and resilient to the challenges you face. You won't get everything right, and sometimes you'll need to act the opposite of how you are feeling, so you need to be aware of what you need to recharge the batteries.

In his book 'The infinite Game' Simon Sinek talks about leadership as not something you win at and having a mindset of winning doesn't help you in the long run. It's best to have an infinite mindset that you are on a path that never ends but evolves, and you can choose at any time to change that path.

Being a leader developer means you are committed to developing your people, so that should be your measure of success. For each key role in your business, you should have a successor in mind who you are developing to have the right skills and attitudes to take responsibility when the time is right.

Summary

Slow down to speed up
The Change Curve
Influencing Styles
When things aren't working out
How far have you come?
Listening, the underrated skill
Motivated Job Chats
Practice doesn't make perfect
For extra resources visit **www.motivatedthebook.com**

Energise

CHAPTER 9:

Energise – Empower Your Team

Introduction

Selling a concept to another person is dependent on our ability to transfer the energy and enthusiasm we have to the other person. Creating a motivated team is all about keeping the levels of energy high driven by a connection to the vision of the business and the personal motivations of the individual.

Something to remember is when we ask someone to do something for us, they will want to know what's in it for them. This is more than just offering a carrot or stick to get them to do what you want them to do, it's about them wanting to do it for their own reasons as well as being connected to the business vision.

If you feel that you are having to push harder than you think you should, then this chapter will help you to fine-tune your approach. To gain commitment, we need to set goals that are perceived as worthwhile and achievable.

Fostering a Team mentality

We've all seen the power of a team in sport, non-more so than when the underdog beats the overwhelming favourite in a cup competition. So, what enables an apparently less able or talented team to beat a much stronger team? Maybe it's because they are a real team as opposed to a group of individuals.

A true team is more than just a group that's been brought together to perform a particular function; they have an interdependence on one another and know what their role and responsibilities are to the team. So, the point of a team is to be able to achieve more together than would be possible separately, T.E.A.M together each achieves more.

Building a team is not easy, it takes commitment and also often a short term loss of performance until you clarify everyone's role and they develop the skills they need. Teams need specialists, kind of like in football, where strikers are required to put the ball in the goal, and a goalkeeper is needed (at the other end) to keep the ball out of the net.

A team also needs structure and a clear purpose that is recognised by the business as a whole or, as James Sale calls it in his book 'Mapping Motivation for top-performing teams', "*the remit*". If we continue the sporting analogy, a team needs to know what it's aiming to achieve, win the cup or league. Is that at all cost, or are there some values we hold dear that we must adhere to, playing by the rules of the game for instance.

Another thing a team needs is a belief in the need to be a team, if this is missing, then every attempt to create a team is likely to fail. Getting the right people with the right balance of skills that are motivated by their role in the team and recognising the need for the other team members are the key elements to getting it right.

Your role as a business owner is to make sure everyone knows the role they play for the team, encourage an ethos of supporting one another, nipping any issues in the bud and celebrating achievements, large and small.

Reward Strategies

Long gone are the days when a good salary will be enough to keep someone happy and engaged at work. To be motivated in our role, we need to have our motivations fulfilled by rewards that mean something to us. When creating a motivated team, we need to have a strategy around what each team member wants from their role.

When I was running my retail business, I was well aware that the rates of pay we could afford to pay were not particularly high so there had to be other reasons why someone would want to work for us.

The majority of our staff were part-time and were either in education, or they were working for a second income for their household. We recognised that one thing they wanted was regular hours so they could plan their diaries with a degree of certainty, so everyone had set days and hours that they always worked.

I didn't think of it as part of our reward strategies at the time but looking back, it had a big part to play in keeping our staff from leaving because, as I've learnt from my work with motivation, certainty is a powerful driver and the lack of it can become demotivating.

It's important to recognise that coming to work is also an opportunity to socialise with other people and feel a sense of belonging. We organised social events and encouraged the input of ideas that would improve the service we offered our customers, both of which fulfilled the need for belonging and contribution.

Having a regular pattern of work and belonging were not important to me, so I had to recognise that my own preferences shouldn't get in the way of giving my team what they wanted. This is where a high level of emotional awareness is key, know what others want even though it goes against your own preferences.

Having a variety of different rewards is essential so there is a choice, it's important to bear in mind that some rewards can be regarded as a punishment to some people. Let's take giving someone an award that they have to go up in front of everyone to receive it; this could have the opposite effect and demotivate someone who doesn't like the limelight.

Training is an effective reward for those who want to be specialists in their role and can be cost-effective for the business if the increased knowledge leads to being able to offer higher-value services. Giving a day off for those who value freedom instead of a bonus can also be cost-effective and motivating for the team member.

It's important to have a variety of options that appeal to a wide variety of motivations for your team to choose from. Don't underestimate the value of good communication about how the business is doing because that will be well received by those driven by security.

Avoid the biggest cog trap

Do you feel that if you stop, everything around you will grind to a halt? This is what I call the biggest cog syndrome, and it's a trap that is easy to fall into. Your business could be doing very well, but the burden on you means you are constantly working hard to keep things going.

The mindset I want you to adopt is that of being the oil that keeps the business running smoothly rather than the biggest cog. Your business needs you not as the biggest working part but as someone who troubleshoots, introduces new ideas, recruits the right people and energises everyone to perform at their best.

The place to start is to ask, what functions in your business are you doing that someone else could easily do with a bit of training? I was guilty of spending too much time ordering stock; after introducing electronic stock control, I became too focused on keeping the stockholding down which led to me spending too much time at my desk.

It can feel uncomfortable to give up a task that you do well and makes you feel like you are making a worthwhile contribution. What can often stop you from making the decision is that the things you should be doing are not easily measured so you can't see you're making a difference.

Don't measure your effectiveness by the number of hours you are working, measure it by what you don't have to do. You should be working to make yourself as redundant as possible because that is when you are being the most effective in leading your business.

Ask your team for feedback

I've covered feedback several times in this book and how important it is to allow us to learn and grow. Asking for feedback from your team is a powerful way to check in with how you are being perceived by those you are leading and it makes them feel their opinion is important.

If this feels like a step too far, you must ask yourself, what is holding me back or what am I avoiding? This is a test of your self-concept, how you see yourself and will take you out of your comfort zone, but you may well be pleasantly surprised by the results.

Our natural instinct is to think we are going to get criticism, but in actual fact, most will be complimentary, and we dismiss it and only focus on the negative. If we receive twenty positive feedback comments and one negative, human nature makes us focus only on the negative and forget the positive.

The simplest way to ask for feedback is just to ask, "How can I help you?" by showing an interest and genuinely wanting to help, you will open up communication. Don't make the mistake I made and assume that because the door is open they will ask if they need help.

You can use questionnaires to gather feedback on how you handle certain situations and what people see as your strengths and weaknesses. The important thing is to use them consistently and not only when there is a problem and tension in the team.

If you are asking for feedback from your team, you are sending a clear message that you know you're not perfect and would like to improve. When I'm working with new managers, it's often the managing up that they struggle with most; you can make it easier by asking and listening.

Are you walking the walk?

Leading a team is about showing the way, not pointing the way, you have to be seen to be walking the walk. If you are asking someone to do something that you wouldn't do yourself, then you are not setting an example to follow.

This is something to be especially aware of as a business owner because there probably isn't anyone going to call you out on it. Although it's important to be doing things that motivate us, we need to be consciously aware of how they may trip us up.

Let's take a couple of examples of typically high or low motivators that could lead to a situation of not walking the walk. Creativity is often an important motivator for entrepreneurs, and one that's often not important is belonging.

In the case of creativity, it's very much around new things and innovation, which is a good thing for a business. Where it can lead to a problem is when it is change for change sake. Not following through and completing things is a common creative trait that can send the wrong message to the team.

In the case of a low drive for belonging, you could be talking about the importance of working together as a team, but your actions are more in line with working autonomously rather than creating a feeling of belonging. This is even more likely to be a problem if one of your top motivators is freedom and autonomy but is easily avoided if you are consciously aware.

The Reluctant Leader Academy was born out of my own experience of ending up in charge of a business and then spending most of my time doing what didn't motivate me and not spending enough time doing the things that did. What's important to remember is that motivations will change depending on our circumstances and future aspirations.

Remaining Enthusiastic

Leading a team is fundamentally a transfer of energy, and, as we have already covered in this book, motivation is the energy we need to perform at our best. When we are motivated, what people see is our enthusiasm for what we are doing, which can act as a magnet that draws people to us.

I am sure you know people who you are naturally attracted to because they have a glow about them that makes you what to spend time with them. We should aspire to be one of those people who brings energy and enthusiasm to every situation.

Remaining enthusiastic is essential for our well-being and for your team that needs to draw on your energy at work. On a scale of 1-10, how enthusiastic are you about what you do in the business? Is it on the way up or starting to slip away?

Your motivations are ever-changing so you need to keep in touch with the ebb and flow of where you get your energy. If you've experienced a lot of change in your life recently, then what's important to you may well have changed. I'm writing this book in the first half of 2021, with the worldwide COVID epidemic still causing much disruption and many challenges which will have changed how many see their future prospects.

It's also worth remembering that a lack of something that doesn't normally motivate us for an extended length of time can become demotivating. Frederick Herzberg called this the 'hygiene theory', nobody goes to work because the washroom is clean, but if it's dirty for a prolonged period of time, it can become a demotivating issue.

If your enthusiasm is dropping, check-in with what's lacking that you can easily address; giving yourself a bit of time away from the business or simply tidying your workspace could give you back your spark.

Everyone wants to make a difference

Over the years of identifying what is motivating my clients and their teams I've noticed how important making a difference is becoming for all age groups. I don't think I was particularly focused on making a difference when I was in my twenties, it was more about creating security and increasing my income.

There are many theories around why making a difference or having purpose is becoming ever more important; I think it's down to us all being far more aware of what's going on in the world. There's hardly a news bulletin nowadays that doesn't mention global warming or another environmental challenge we have to tackle.

If you are running a business, it's important to consider what this means to how you communicate with your clients, suppliers and your employees. We have looked at the importance of motivation, our 'Why', for our own performance and so we should consider why someone would buy from us, supply us or work for us.

Your customers are becoming more and more savvy when it comes to how they spend their money, so we should make sure our marketing includes why we do what we do. Our story, which we covered in chapter one, has an important role to play. How we go about things, our values, and a connection to a cause that's much bigger than we could change on our own, are all good ways to tap into the difference we make.

Your team will want to be connected to the outcome that you deliver to your customers and how you help them overcome a problem by what you do. This is quite often missed by businesses that are financial or task-focused, the remedy is to focus on how and what you are communicating back to your employees.

If there is a clear driving purpose for the work you do, then you are more likely to be able to ride the tough times and not throw in the towel at the first sign of difficulty. Having a clear purpose will, in the long run, save you money by recruiting the right people who want to contribute to your purpose, and the reduction in staff turnover will save on recruiting and training costs.

Looking back to our retail business, my father had a clear purpose to build a business to pass on to the next generation and provide the best shopping experience to our local community. When we bought my father out of the business, we continued to grow the business in line with those values with a view to pass on to the next generation.

It's a good idea when someone who has had a big influence on the business leaves to revisit the vision to see whether it is still relevant. We adapted our vision in the knowledge that our children had shown no interest in working in the business.

Transferring responsibility

Showing you have trust in your team and giving them responsibilities is an essential part of creating a business that sets you free. You can't do everything, and if you could, it wouldn't be a business, it would be a job, so you need to be able to successfully pass over responsibility.

This is more than a logical step, it's also a big emotional step; if you've had children, it's like the first time you leave your baby with someone else. It's important to recognise the emotional pushback you are likely to feel and the voice in your head that's telling you it's not worth the hassle.

Having high expectations is essential, and we have already covered the secret of explicitness, which is essential when communicating what you want, how you want it to be done and why. It's also important to have high expectations for everyone in your team and being consistent in how you show up.

When we are passing over responsibility, it's not a case of 'here you go, it's yours now'; it should be that you now see yourself as a supporting figure that keeps morale high. As William C Byham wrote in his book 'Zapp! The lightning power of empowerment', "*we should be injecting Zapp into the team and not becoming a sap.*"

It's easy to fall into the trap of only picking up on mistakes, coming down hard on them and ignoring the good things that have happened. This can often be driven by an ego reaction that believes 'they can't do without me, and I've found more evidence to prove that is the case'.

When my father left our retail business, he commented that he didn't think the business would continue to be successful without him. I don't think that he said this because he thought we weren't capable, more that we would have to learn to work together without him.

Developing people has to be the mantra if you are going to build a team that is capable and motivated to take responsibilities away from you. By focusing on the skills they need to do their job and keeping them motivated, you will create a team that will set you free.

Summary
Fostering a team mentality
Reward Strategies
Avoid being the biggest cog
Ask your team for feedback
Are you walking the walk?
Remaining Enthusiastic
Everyone wants to make a difference
Transferring Responsibilities
For extra resources visit **www.motivatedthebook.com**

Conclusion

Being a business owner has many challenges, and at times you are bound to wonder why you bother, so maintaining our energy levels is essential. Whether you are just starting out or have been running your business for many years, your energy levels will be key to your success.

A business is a journey, not a destination, make sure you enjoy the journey and make conscious decisions about the direction you want to go. Maintain a positive mindset that is growth-focused, accepting that not everything will go with your plan and everything is an opportunity to learn.

Pick the role in the business you really want and delegate the rest as soon as you can, you don't have to be managing director unless you want to be. Take the time to write your own job description that sets out your role and your responsibilities to the business and the team. This should stop you from carrying out tasks that are not your responsibility, even if you do find them easy.

Look after your well-being by making sure you are eating well, taking regular exercise, and prioritising your sleep. You are vital for the business so you need to look after number one, don't sacrifice your health for the sake of the business; treat yourself as you would your best friend.

I've taken you through the seven-step M.E.A.S.U.R.E model that starts with holding up the mirror so you understand how you show up and how to play to your strengths. This step is easy to skip but will come back to bite you sooner or later; your skills are important but so is having a high level of self-awareness and emotional intelligence.

The next step is to create a business that motivates you, this is where the Evaluate, Action and Systemise steps fit in. Finally, the last three steps of Unify, Review and Energise are where you create your Motivated team to carry on your vision.

Every business that has ever been started was set up to solve a problem, staying focused on what that problem is will stop you from getting side-tracked. It's easy to watch what your competitors are doing and get fixated on being the same and ending up doing something you never set out to do.

Having said that, you can change the problem you solve whenever you choose, the important thing to remember is to be clear and explicit in the three things that matter, what you do, how you do it and why it matters.

If your business is to set you free, then developing the right team will ultimately do that, your role is to be the developer of that team. A top-performing team will need to have the skills to do the job and the motivation to want to do it.

In this book, I've shared my journey, what I've learnt along the way, the mistakes I made and knowing now what I know, what I would do differently. Whatever your motivation for being a business owner, make sure you check in with yourself regularly.

Get the three elements of a Motivated You, Motivated Business and a Motivated Team right, and you stand the best chance of creating a business that sets you free!

About the Author

Mark joined his family retail business from school and gradually took over the running of the business from his father. When a national retailer enquired about purchasing the business, it gave Mark the opportunity to start his coaching business.

Mark uses his 30 years of experience and tools he has picked up during his journey to help his business clients to avoid the mistakes he made and fast-track their success.

To connect with Mark visit **www.motivatedthebook.com**

References/Bibliography

Chapter 1
The Attitude Book (Simon Tyler)
The Decision Book (Mikel Krogerus & Roman Tschapppeler)
Watertight Marketing (Bryony Thomas)
The Top 5 Regrets of the Dying (Bronnie Ware)
Change Your Life with NLP (Lindsey Agness)
The Mindfulness Book (Martyn Newman)

Chapter 2
24/6 The Power of Unplugging One Day A Week (Tiffany Shlain)
The productivity of working hours 2014 Stanford University
The Business of Sleep (Vicki Culpin)
How to Have the Energy (Graham Alcott & Colette Heneghan)
Better Then Before (Gretchen Rubin)
Atomic Habits (James Clear)
The Feedback Book (Dawn Sillett)
Johari Window
(Pioneering Professional, D Biddle & A Stewart)
Mindset (Carol Dweck)
Character Strengths and Virtues (Christopher Peterson & Martin Seligman)
Engaging for Success, The Macleod Report (David Macleod and Nita Clarke)

Chapter 3
Psychological Types (Dr Carl G Jung)
C-me Colour Profiling (**www.colour-profiling.com**)
Mapping Motivation (James Sale)
Motivational Maps (**www.motivationalmaps.com**)
The Gifts of Imperfection (Brene Brown)

Liberating Leadership (Dr Derek Biddle & Ali Stewart)
Rocket Fuel (Gino Wickman & Mark C Winters)
The Art of Possibility (Rosalind & Benjamin Zander)

Chapter 4
The Crossroads Model from The Decision Book (Mikel Krogerus & Roman Tschapppeler)
Mapping Motivation for Leadership (James Sale & Jane Thomas)
The Seven Habits of Highly Effective People (Stephen Covey)
Start with Why (Simon Sinek)
The Business Model Canvas
(**www.strategyzer.com/canvas/business-model-canvas**)
They Ask You Answer (Marcus Sheridan)
Who Not How (Dan Sullivan & Dr Benjamin Hardy)
Good to Great (Jim Collins)

Chapter 5
The E-Myth Revisited (Michael E Gerber)
Liberating Leadership (Dr Derek Biddle & Ali Stewart)
The Onion Model
Transactional Analysis (Eric Berne)
The Gifts of imperfection (Brene Brown)

Chapter 6
Measure What Matters (John Doerr)
Pareto Principle (Vilfredo Pareto)
Mapping Motivation for Leadership (James Sale & Jane Thomas)
VIA Character Strengths Assessment
(**www.viacharacter.org)**

Chapter 7
Tribes (Seth Godin)

Building A Story Brand (Donald Miller)
Liberating Leadership (Dr Derek Biddle & Ali Stewart)
The Ego is The Enemy (Ryan Holiday)

Chapter 8
The Change Curve
Liberating Leadership (Dr Derek Biddle & Ali Stewart)
The Seven Habits of Highly Effective People (Stephen Covey)
The Infinite Game (Simon Sinek)

Chapter 9
Mapping Motivation for Top Performing Teams (James Sale)
Zapp! The Lightning Power of Empowerment (William C Byham)

Printed in Great Britain
by Amazon

75425267R00102